Madame Benoit's LAMB COOKBOOK

Madame Benoit's
LAMB
COOKBOOK

Mme. Jehane Benoit

McGraw-Hill Ryerson Limited

Toronto   Montreal   New York   St. Louis   San Francisco   Auckland
Beirut   Bogotá   Düsseldorf   Johannesburg   Lisbon   London   Lucerne
Madrid   Mexico   New Delhi   Panama   Paris   San Juan
São Paulo   Singapore   Sydney   Tokyo

MADAME BENOIT'S LAMB COOK BOOK

ISBN 0-07-082944-6

1 2 3 4 5 6 7 8 9 10 BP 8 7 6 5 4 3 2 1 0 9

Printed and bound in Canada

Photography by René Delbuguet

Canadian Cataloguing in Publication Data

Benoit, Jehane, date
    Madame Benoit's lamb cook book

Includes index.
ISBN 0-07-082944-6

1. Cookery (Lamb and mutton)   I. Title.
II. Title: Lamb cook book.

TX749.B45   641.6'6'3   C79-094226-7

To my husband, Bernard, who has found enough hours in each day through the years to make our own sheep farm a reality, and to my publisher for their faith and understanding about my interest in lamb.

Acknowledgments

I wish to express my deep appreciation to John C. Ross, secretary-manager of the Canada Sheep Council for his courteous attention to my requests for help and advice. I would also like to thank the Council itself for its kind permission to adapt illustrations and use photographs, and for its unfailing support in promoting lamb across the country. Special thanks are due to various people in the Alberta Department of Agriculture, in particular to Lorraine Rea, who persuaded me that the time was right for a lamb cook book. To Lalovee Jensen, the first chairman of the Canada Sheep Council, and to the many devoted sheep farmers I have met in my travels across the country, I express my thanks for their encouragement and support in writing this book.

Contents

Introduction

Why lamb? It is my preference for lamb over all other meat, both for cooking and eating, that made me write a book on cooking lamb. I hope to encourage more people to cook and eat it in many ways, to make use of the numerous cuts available — and even to persuade their butchers to prepare particular cuts they want if they do not already have them. After all, there can be few things more satisfying than feeding one's family and friends with lovingly prepared food.

I feel that I must not leave one rule unwritten when it comes to lamb, and that is this: "Don't overcook young lamb." It must come out of the oven a beautiful pink, and certainly not well done. The first succulent bite should tell you that it's done to perfection. I remember the satisfaction I had, many years ago, in a simple little restaurant in Genoa, Italy, where a large tray was brought in, straight from the oven, filled with gorgeous chunks of lamb roasted a delicate "pink," and surrounded with hot tomatoes, the whole thing flavored with fresh basil and sautéed garlic. The delight of this meal still remains with me. This is what I mean by that "first succulent bite" one never forgets.

My own very special interest in lamb comes from the fact that more than twenty years ago, my husband, Bernard, and I bought a sheep farm in the Eastern Townships of Quebec, near the beautiful mountains of Vermont. One of the great joys of our lives has been the pleasure of living in the country, at "Noirmouton," and raising our sheep. We used to live in Montreal before that, and came to live in the country — strange as it may sound — because of my husband's passion for sports cars. Every spring seemed to bring a new model, and one particular year, a new one had to be tried once again. We often came to the part of the Eastern Townships near where we now live, because we found the mountains so beautiful, and this is where Bernard tested the speed of his car. However, he soon discovered he was being followed by the police, so he made a quick turn onto a little road, thinking he'd been very clever and left the police car far behind. But the officer was having the last laugh — he had stopped following because he knew it would be that narrow, bumpy little road that would stop Bernard. That's not all, though. As he slowed down, Bernard saw a "For Sale" sign on a piece of property, stopped the car, got out, and was so won over by the beauty of the surroundings that he quickly turned back to the village, looked for the agent, and right then and there bought the farm.

Of course, in his excitement, Bernard didn't notice that the house was unsightly — dirty and badly in need of repair! However, we built our own surroundings, fixing up the house and outbuildings, while gradually becoming aware of the give and take in nature's cycle, and we learned to become a part of it. Both of us wanted to create some new life around us, and it just naturally came to us, as if we had planned it all along, that what we wanted was to create a very good sheep farm. What we did *not* know, of course, was how much hard work — and money — it would take. But somehow we have never felt we would like to give it up.

Lamb, of course, goes back to the days of the bible and beyond, and it was this strong sense of tradition that appealed to both of us. In my romantic way, I could see our farm with woods and rolling green meadows, babbling brooks, an old stone house, a little chapel, a garden of roses (that goats never eat), and beautiful little lambs as I imagined they must have looked in the days of the bible, enjoying it all as much as I did. What I forgot was that a babbling brook could not run before it was cleaned of the debris from years of negligence, that roses took time to grow and great care so frost (or goats) would not make them disappear, that the stone house wasn't feasible, and that those "biblical" little lambs came into the world during the worst cold or storms just as human babies seem to. We also didn't realize that sheep have to be fed, watered and cared for every day, that to help keep wild animals from killing the lambs we would need good dogs, and that they must also be fed and housed, and cuddled as well.

Sometimes we have wondered whether it has been worth the effort. But we think a moment, and look around us, and then we really do know that it is worth all the work we put into it. We have our chickens, and they give us lots of big tasty eggs for all the family. Each spring, I enjoy seeing them go wild searching for fresh bugs as they hatch; they cackle and make a wonderful "coricocou" sound as they run about. After all, living in the country and breeding sheep is a whole way of life, so to do it you must have a real desire to create a pleasant environment so all your hours of work can be as rewarding as possible.

On sunny summer mornings when I look out at our flock of lambs grazing in the green meadow, I cannot help but think they are part of that very long line of the most amenable animals man has ever known, hailing perhaps from the arid southern soil of far-away ancient Egypt. Since I'm a real romantic, this thought gives me pleasure and a deep sense of peace and timelessness. If you are interested in the many cultures of the world and are curious about our own food heritage, you will be fascinated by the history of how man domesticated sheep through the ages. Norman Kees, a British researcher on the origin of domesticated animals, has concluded that large cattle were first tamed and raised in the Nile delta area of ancient Egypt, because of its fertile land and available water. Sheep and goats (or "small cattle" as they were called) seem to have first appeared in the southern regions of Egypt where they preferred (as they do today) the arid conditions and stubby, coarse pasture. The fact that we still find archaeological evidence of ram worship in the south of Egypt supports this opinion.

It is difficult to determine exactly when domesticated sheep first appeared in the life of man, since early Pre-Dynastic drawings of long-horn sheep on cliffs along the Nile Valley, and drawings found among the Neolithic desert rocks provide still more proof that they have long been part of human civilization. It would seem that sheep were domesticated once nomads became farmers. To look at them, you wouldn't think the wild sheep of ancient Egypt, with its massive horns and long, silky mane, nor the European *mouflon,* which looked very much like our wild mountain sheep, were related to the wooly little lambs we have today. Yet, it is this same family of "little cattle" that has given birth to hundreds of breeds of sheep that have since bleated their patient paths across every country on earth. But however much they have changed in appearance down through the centuries, the behavior of sheep (unlike that of cows and horses) hasn't changed much at all.

The symbols of sheep and lambs are closely entwined in religious and holy allegory, and in folklore and legend all over the world. It is a young lamb that was tucked protectively under the Good Shepherd's arm and wrapped around his neck to give him warmth in the cool night air of the desert. (Even today, nomads still do the same.)

Of course, sheep and lambs were revered in the early life of man because they provided him with many of his needs: wool, milk, butter, cheese and meat. In ancient times, large pieces of lamb were fire-grilled in large braziers and offered on pieces of hard bread or in deep iron plates and eaten with the hands. In Renaissance Italy, elegant dinners were the fashion and their influence spread from Florence, Bologna and other cities to France and beyond. Italian cooks become highly sought-after in the great houses of the day. Often, their *pièce de résistance* was roast lamb, which they prided themselves in being able to cook better than anyone else.

Let me close by quoting the great chef, Escoffier: "When entertaining one's friends, one should have the same sort of food one has all the time — only more of it." With me it is braised lamb shanks or broiled lamb chops, or a good lamb curry, or one of a host of good lamb dishes. But it is definitely *lamb.* It is my hope that you enjoy it too.

Jehane Benoit

1

What You Should Know About Lamb

Lamb is the meat of sheep under one year of age. Any meat from a sheep older than one year is called mutton. Genuine spring lamb, early lamb or "weaned" lamb, as it is referred to, can be purchased any time between March and September. Anyone wanting to enjoy lamb all year round can purchase lamb carcasses (cut, labelled, and fast-frozen) during lamb's prime times, in summer and early autumn, then stock their freezer with first-quality meat. Through my own experience, I can assure you that lamb will keep 6 to 9 months in perfect condition in the average home freezer.

What to Look for in Selecting Cuts of Lamb

Color and Texture

Young lamb will have bright, pink flesh and pure white fat, with soft, moist, pinkish bones. The lean part is firm to the touch, never flabby or tough.

Weight

The weight of the leg of lamb is a good indication of the quality and age of the animal. The leg should be 4 to 5 lb. (2–2.5 kg) and never exceed 7 lb. (3.5 kg). If the leg is heavier than that, it is from a mature lamb, and its meat will not be as delicately flavored, nor as tender as meat from a young lamb.

The Cuts

An entire lamb carcass weighs from 40 to 60 lb. (20–30 kg). The butcher divides it across the back in two equal sections, the Fore Quarter (the neck end) and the Hind Quarter (the leg).

The Fore Quarter is divided in the following way:

The Neck: Cut just in front of the shoulder, usually 1 in. (2.5 cm) thick. This is a tender and tasty meat, perfect for moist cooking (casserole type) or for making lamb stock (use the leftover cooked meat to make hash or salad).

The Shoulder: In the language of the butcher, the front leg of the lamb is called the shoulder. It is not as tender as the leg from the back, which is the true leg of lamb; but it is very tasty and can be prepared in many ways. Out of the shoulder are cut the blade steaks, the ones with the long bones, and arm steaks, the ones with the round bone. Often these are part of "lamb-in-the-basket," found at supermarket counters.

A boned and rolled lamb shoulder is an economical buy. It is tender and makes an excellent roast. However, when the bones are left in, the roast is equally good, though very difficult to carve. The best methods of cooking an unrolled shoulder are braising or pot roasting, and poaching. Cut in pieces, it can be the base of many an elegant and tasty stew or casserole. A 3 to 5 lb. (1.5–2.25) rolled shoulder, roasted at 325–350°F. (165–180°C) will need 20 to 25 minutes per lb. (0.5 kg) for medium rare. On the meat thermometer, use the same temperature for rare, medium or well-done as for a roasted leg of lamb.

To make a fancy cut with the shoulder, some specialized butchers will make a cushion shoulder — partly boned and tied on two sides, it forms a sort of square cushion. These should be roasted. There is also the square cut shoulder, which takes its name from its shape; it is unboned, and the blade and arm steaks have been removed. These can be roasted, poached or braised.

The Breast is the end cut of the shoulder and is tender and very tasty. It is sometimes cut and trimmed like a square of pork sparerib (and cooked in the same manner) or in riblets, perfect for a summer barbecue or for broiling in the oven; they usually take 10 to 12 minutes per side. Cooks in many Central European countries make something very special with the riblets. They are boned, quickly charcoal-broiled, and served very hot with a spicy sauce — delicious. Rolled, then boiled with an assortment of vegetables cooked in its broth, the breast makes a very interesting cold cut when it is cooked and cooled. When boned and stuffed with any favorite type of stuffing, this cut can be roasted in a 300°F. (150°C) oven, and lightly covered with a square of foil paper. It's at its best served hot.

The Fore Shanks are the two front legs of the lamb. They tend to be fatty and contain a good deal of connective tissue, but at the same time are quite meaty and tender. It is worth the effort of looking for lamb shanks because not only are they very good, but they also make an attractive individual portion size, especially when they are from a very small, young lamb. When they are a little larger, you can ask your butcher to cut them in two. They are very adaptable to any recipe that calls for a long, slow, moist type of cooking.

The Hind Quarter contains the rib, the loin and the leg, all high-quality cuts. There is also the flank, which is of lower quality, and is generally ground for meat patties.

The Rack or Rib Roast comes from the rib section which can be cut in 6 or 8 ribs, or 12 ribs all in one piece for roasting. It is tender and delicately flavored, with very little gristle. The first 4 to 5 chops cut from the front of the rib section, or nearest the loin, are the very best.

The Crown Roast is prepared with the 2-rib rack, shaped and tied in the shape of a crown. The tops of the rib bones are scraped of meat or "Frenched," as it is called, and the center is usually filled with a stuffing before roasting. This is an elegant cut, more costly than the plain rib rack, because of the extra work involved for the butcher, yet it is not really any better than the other — it's done largely as a show piece.

Loin Chops These are the most tender chops of all. They have a small T-bone that separates the tenderloin from the "eye." Loin chops can also have the kidney inserted; in this case, it fits neatly below the tenderloin and the tail is then curved around it and secured with a skewer. When the same chop is boned and rolled, it becomes a *noisette*. A *noisette* of lamb should be 2 in. (5 cm) thick.

English Lamb Chops These are used for special dinners. They are considered quite a delicacy.
    The saddle (the two loins unseparated) is simply cut into individual double chops 1½ in. (4 cm) thick, then the tails are tucked around to form a circle of meat, which then has two T-bones, two tenderloins and two eyes.

Honey-Glazed Leg of Lamb
The combination of honey and mustard gives the skin a crusty texture and makes a deep brown gravy with a delectable flavor.

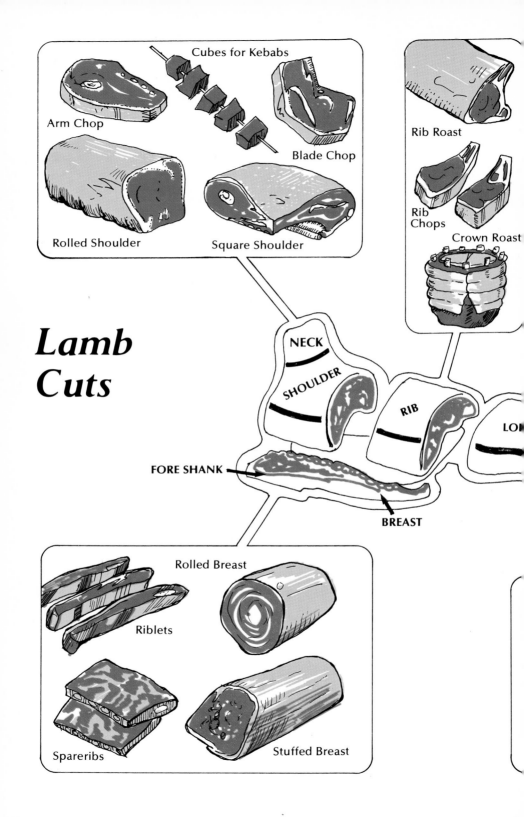

Cubes for Kebabs

Arm Chop

Blade Chop

Rolled Shoulder

Square Shoulder

Rib Roast

Rib Chops

Crown Roast

Lamb Cuts

NECK

SHOULDER

RIB

LO

FORE SHANK

BREAST

Rolled Breast

Riblets

Spareribs

Stuffed Breast

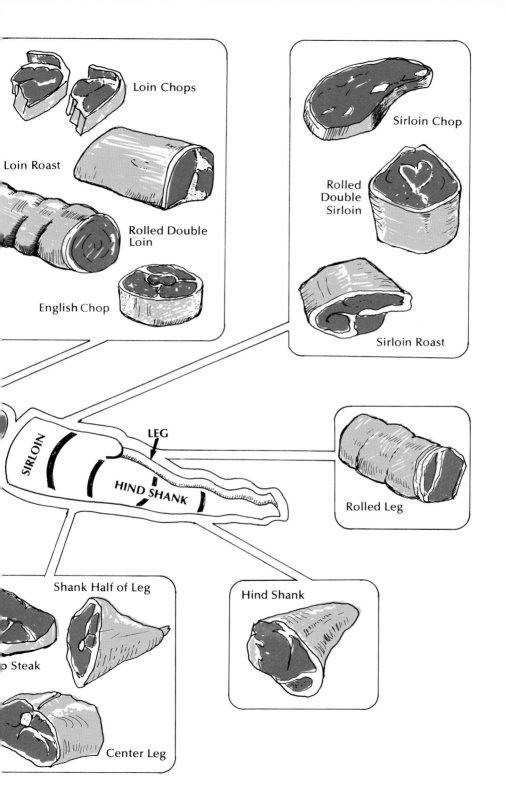

Loin Chops

Loin Roast

Rolled Double Loin

English Chop

Sirloin Chop

Rolled Double Sirloin

Sirloin Roast

SIRLOIN

LEG

HIND SHANK

Rolled Leg

Shank Half of Leg

Hind Shank

Steak

Center Leg

Adapted from Canada Sheep Council chart

Sherried Lamb Casserole
Lamb shanks are tender, tasty and low in cost. They are used in this casserole, one of my favorites for a winter buffet.

Rib Lamb Chops These are the chops cut from the rack which is behind the loin. They have no tenderloin, but are delicious. They can be cut into single, double or triple chops, the best being the double, usually 2 in. (5 cm) thick.

French Rib Chops are the same as regular rib chops, except that the fat is well trimmed and the end bones are left bare. They are usually served with the bone dressed up in frilly paper; this is done so they can be held in the fingers for eating.

Blade Lamb Chops These come from the front of the shoulder, right behind the rack. When well cooked, they are tender and tasty and surely more economical than rib chops.

Shoulder Lamb Chops These are cut from the lower part of the shoulder, near the shank, and they have a small round bone.

Whole Loin of Lamb This includes the loin chops and the rib chops in one piece, or 12 to 14 ribs.

Rack of Lamb This consists of the rib chops behind the loin chops. A rack usually weighs from 1¾ to 2 lb. (0.75–1 kg), a 6-chop rack, which serves two people.

The Saddle Roast or Rolled Double Loin is a luxury cut — both sides of the loins with some bone removed and the flank ends trimmed, then rolled. The saddle is then firmly tied, so it will hold its shape during roasting. To carve a roasted saddle, slice in long horizontal strips, then turn it over and cut into the flank ends, thus reaching the tenderloin.

The Whole Sirloin and Shank Half can be boned and rolled to obtain a complete rolled leg, which is an excellent cut to serve 10 to 14. The shank half of the leg can be roasted, where a small roast is desired to serve 6 to 8. It can also be cut "butterfly," which means completely boned and cooked opened up flat like a steak, and barbecued or broiled in the oven. It takes about 10 minutes per lb. (0.5 kg) to grill, and it is very easy to serve, cut on the bias in long thin slices.

Leg Steaks are cut from between the sirloin part and the top of the shank half of the leg. They are tender and tasty, and can be cooked the same as a steak, rare or medium being the best.

The Center Leg Cut is a roast which is cut from the sirloin end and the top of the shank half and is an excellent roast to serve 4 to 6.

The Hind Shank Roast is a delicious, small roast which is perfect to serve for 2 people.

The Whole Leg can be "Frenched," meaning that 3 to 5 in. (7–12 cm) of the end bone is scraped of all meat, and served with a frill, like a Crown Roast.

American or English Style Leg is a leg with the shank bone cut, and the meat tucked into a pocket on the inside of the leg, and then tied together.

Cooking Lamb the Right Way

Since lamb is an excellent source of high-quality protein, it is worthwhile to learn how to cook it properly. Lamb is easily digested, making its nutrients readily available for body use, and is really a quick-energy meat, ideal for diets of all age groups — and even for weight-watchers since in most cuts the fat is easily separated from the lean.

A roast of lamb is one of the easiest types to cook. Since it is a red meat, like beef, it can be roasted rare, medium or well done, and is at its best rare or medium. It is sometimes seared in a 400°F. (200°C) oven and the roasting finished off at 325°F. (165°C), or it is roasted at an even 350°F. (180°C) temperature for the whole cooking period. Certain recipes require basting, but for others it is not necessary. I cannot too strongly recommend the use of a meat thermometer when roasting lamb, as it is a failproof way to have it cooked perfectly to your taste, regardless of the type of recipe or oven temperature used. Use this as guide:

145°F. (63°C) on the thermometer indicates rare
155°F. (68°C) on the thermometer indicates medium
175°F. (80°C) on the thermometer indicates very well done.

When cooking a half-leg or loin, there is no problem when using a meat thermometer; and since the degree of heat called for when cooking a half-leg is the same as that for a whole leg, it is easy to calculate, even if you do not have a thermometer.

For a good brown crust on top of the roast, it is better to use a shallow roasting pan, about 1½–2½ in. (4–7 cm) high.

Never roast lamb covered, unless specified in the recipe.

A rolled breast or shoulder of lamb will take 1½ to 2 hours to cook in a 325°F. (165°C) oven. A lamb chop 1 in. (2.5 cm) thick will broil in a total time of 12 minutes; a chop 1½ in. (3.75 cm) thick takes 18 minutes; and a chop 2 in. (5 cm) thick takes 22 minutes. Lamb stew should be simmered for 1½ to 2 hours.

Leftover lamb is no problem, as it can be used in a curry, salad, hash, or casserole. Or serve it thickly sliced as a cold cut, but here I have a word of advice: never serve cold lamb just out of the refrigerator — let it stand at room temperature for 2 to 4 hours before cutting, so that the fat will not be hard.

When cooking lamb, a very important point to remember is that whether you are roasting, braising, or stewing it, *do not overcook* it. Often we hear comments such as, "I don't like lamb — it has an unpleasant odor." But the only thing that can cause an odor with lamb is cooking it at too high a temperature, because lamb fat is classed as "hard fat" and burns at a lower degree of heat than other animal fats. To roast lamb, 325°F. (165°C) is the ideal temperature. (Searing can be done, but only for a brief period.) Of course, mutton from a 2 to 3 year-old sheep could have a greasy smell while roasting, but you will not find this problem with a young or spring lamb.

Remember to serve lamb on very hot plates. Again, the reason for this is that the hard fat will coagulate on cold plates. Always keep in mind that the full delicate flavor of lamb can be tasted when it is served piping hot.

Accompaniments

The old familiar dishes appear again and again. We love them because we have been serving them for years, or we dislike them because they seem so repetitious. With lamb, just a few delectable ideas are necessary to keep it an adventure in eating. Please do try some of the following and find out how much they appeal to you.

Glaze a roasting leg or shoulder of lamb in the last 20 minutes of cooking with ¼ cup (60 mL) prepared French mustard, ½ cup (125 mL) honey, 1 tsp. (5 mL) salt, and ½ tsp. (2 mL) pepper mixed together.

Try the Scandinavian idea of basting a roast lamb 3 to 5 times during the cooking period with a cup of *café au lait*. Pour ½ cup (125 mL) of warm milk over ½ cup (125 mL) strong coffee [or 1 tbsp (15 mL) instant coffee for ½ cup (125 mL) of water]. Sweeten with 1 tbsp. (15 mL) honey or brown sugar.

Make a Finnish glaze by basting the roast of lamb, in the last 20 minutes of cooking, with 1 to 1½ cups (250–375 mL) of uncooked chopped lingonberries or cranberries mixed with 1 tbsp. (15 mL) grated lemon rind, the juice of 1 lemon, a pinch of basil, and ½ tsp. (2 mL) ginger.

Mix together 1 can undiluted frozen orange juice, the juice of 1 lemon, ¼ cup (60 mL) soft butter or margarine, and ¼ cup (60 mL) chopped fresh mint. Pour over a leg or boned shoulder of lamb, and roast according to recipe.

Make an Oriental marinade to baste any lamb cuts while broiling or barbecuing. In a jar, combine 1 to 3 crushed cloves garlic, ½ tsp. (2 mL) dry ginger or 1 tbsp. (15 mL) grated fresh ginger, 1 tbsp. (15 mL) honey, ¾ cup (375 mL) soya sauce.

Rosemary, basil, mint and sage (fresh sage, when possible) are the best herbs to use with lamb. Orange and lemon rinds are also very tasty accompaniments.

Another idea is to place on a platter your "butterfly" leg of lamb to be barbecued. Top with as many thinly-sliced onion rings as you like, and sprinkle with crushed peppercorns, salt and rosemary to taste. Cover and refrigerate overnight.

Tie together a bunch of fresh green onions, and use to dip in dry Madeira or dry Port wine, to baste lamb as it broils — superb.

Place in the bowl of your food processor the juice of 1 lemon, 3 green onions cut in four (the white and the green), 1 heaping tbsp. (15 mL) each of chutney and peanut butter, ¼ tsp. (1 mL) freshly ground pepper, and ¼ cup (60 mL) olive or vegetable oil. Process off and on until creamy. Brush on roast or chops before broiling or barbecuing or roasting.

For tasty kebabs, brush the following on top, 8 to 10 minutes before cooking is finished: stir together ½ cup (125 mL) dry sherry or Port, ⅔ cup (165 mL) canned apricot or peach nectar, 2 tbsp. (30 mL) brown sugar, and a pinch each of curry powder and mace.

Make this French chef's glaze to brush on your roast or chop or lamb riblet. Shake together ¾ cup (185 mL) black currant jelly or Seville orange (bitter) marmalade and ½ cup (125 mL) red wine vinegar.

Serve roast or chops with curried green peas. Add to canned peas half the water in the can, 1 tbsp. (15 mL) butter blended with 2 tsp. (10 mL) flour and 1 tsp. (5 mL) curry. Stir together over low heat until creamy and hot. Salt to taste and serve.

This is a superb chutney to serve with lamb, one that will keep for months refrigerated. Soak ¼ cup (60 mL) dry currants in ¼ cup (60 mL) Port wine for 1 hour. Pour in a sauce pan and simmer over low heat about 15 to 20 minutes. Pour hot into 1 cup (250 mL) chutney of your choice, and stir to mix. Add 1 tsp. (5 mL) ground fenugreek (optional).

Make a hot English cucumber sauce to serve with a roast of lamb, instead of gravy. Peel and chop a medium-sized cucumber, and boil 15 minutes in ½ cup (125 mL) chicken stock. Pass through a sieve or into the food processor to purée. Beat the yolk of 1 egg into the sauce until it thickens. Sometimes the sauce is hot enough to thicken naturally or simmer while stirring over low heat. Don't let it boil or it will curdle. Add the grated rind of 1 lemon and 1 tbsp. (15 mL) fresh lemon juice and salt to taste.

As a last word, here are four of my favorite wines to serve with lamb. They are fairly costly, but so good:

Clos René Pomerol, 1964 (French, light red)
Corton Clos du Roi, 1962 (Burgundy)
Valpolicella Bertani (Italian, dry red)
Chianti Barelo (Italian, medium-dry red).

2   Ground Lamb

Since ground lamb can be prepared in so many ways, it will help you create appetizing, low-cost and nutritious meals, and at the same time add a little glamour to your dishes by using a different meat than you usually do.

When ground lamb is not available, buy what is called "lamb-in-a-basket." Remove the meat from the bones and put it through a meat grinder once or twice, or grind in a food processor or blender, ½ lb. (0.25 kg) at a time for 30–40 seconds each time. Don't discard the bones — use them to make a delicious lamb broth (see Leftovers section).

My Family Lamburger

I sometimes get a bit tired of ground beef for burgers, so it's a pleasure to use ground lamb. The following recipe is my family's favorite.

> 1½–2 lb. (0.75–1 kg) ground lamb
> ½ tsp. (2 mL) onion or garlic salt
> ½ cup (125 mL) chopped green onions
> 4 tbsp. (60 mL) dry sherry or fresh lemon juice
> 1 tsp. (5 mL) salt
> ½ tsp. (2 mL) sugar
> ¼ tsp. (1 mL) pepper
> ½ tsp. (2 mL) ground basil or thyme
> Paprika

Mix all ingredients together thoroughly. Gently shape, without packing, into patties. Sprinkle with paprika. Broil in a preheated broiler 3 in. (7.5 cm) from the source of heat for 6 to 8 minutes on each side. These patties are at their best when cooked slightly rare. (They can also be cooked in a cast-iron frying pan, the same way you do hamburgers.) *Serves 6–8.*

Cocktail Marbles

An interesting hot tidbit for a party. Cook them in the morning; and when they are ready to serve, heat the plum sauce in a chafing dish or an electric frying pan, add the meat balls and stir around as indicated in the recipe.

2 lb. (1 kg) ground lamb
½ cup (125 mL) Japanese soy sauce
2 cloves garlic, chopped fine
1 tbsp. (15 mL) vegetable oil
⅔ cup (165 mL) Oriental plum sauce

Mix together thoroughly in a bowl the ground lamb, soy sauce and garlic. Shape into large marble-size balls. Heat oil in a large frying pan. When hot, add as many meat balls as it will take without crowding.

Cook over high heat. Shake the pan to toss them around so they brown all over, and remove to a platter with a slotted spoon. Repeat this operation until they are all browned (usually no more oil need be added after the first time). Only a few minutes are needed to cook them. Do not refrigerate.

When ready to serve, warm up the plum sauce. Add all the meat balls at once and cook over low heat for 5 minutes, or until hot and glazed. Serve with wooden picks. *Serves 10–12.*

English Lamb Patties

This is a recipe that was given to me in 1963 by the chef at the Connaught Hotel in London, England, where the food has always been superbly cooked and served. Even though these patties are really a sort of lamburger, the currant jelly, capers and Madeira wine combine to give them the personality of the chef, a touch that makes them something very special.

> 1½–2 lb (0.75–1 kg) ground lamb
> 1 small onion, finely chopped
> 2 tsp. (10 mL) salt
> 1 tbsp. (15 mL) capers
> 1 tbsp. (15 mL) butter
> 1 tsp. (5 mL) vegetable oil
> ⅓ cup (80 mL) black currant jelly or jam
> 3 tbsp. (50 mL) dry Madeira or Port wine

Mix together in a bowl the lamb, onion, salt and capers. Shape into patties about 1 in. (2.5 cm) thick.

Heat butter and oil together in a cast-iron frying pan until it becomes a nutty color. Add patties and brown on both sides, over medium heat, about 6 minutes on each side, turning only once. Drain out most of the fat. Then add the currant jelly or jam and stir gently. Cover the pan and cook over very low heat for 5 minutes, stirring just once. (This will glaze the patties.) Remove patties to a hot platter. Add the Madeira or Port wine to juice remaining in pan. Stir around while scraping bottom of pan, and pour over meat. *Serves 6.*

Moroccan Meat Patties

I strongly recommend these for a successful barbecue party. The spicing is unusual, but not exotic. I like to serve them on broken pieces of buttered pita bread.

2 lb. (1 kg) ground lamb
2 slices white bread with crusts removed
1 clove garlic, chopped fine
½ tsp. (2 mL) ground cumin
2 tbsp. (30 mL) chili sauce or ketchup
2 tsp. (10 mL) paprika
1 tsp. (5 mL) salt
¼ tsp. (1 mL) ground fenugreek (optional)
¼ tsp. (1 mL) ground allspice
1 egg, lightly beaten
2 tbsp. (30 mL) chopped parsley

Pound the ground lamb and bread in a pestal and mortar, or in a bowl with a large spoon, or grind twice in a meat grinder. Add all the remaining ingredients and thoroughly mix with wet hands. The secret of success is in the grinding and mixing of the mixture until it becomes a paste. Form into patties, and broil over charcoal or in the broiler, 3 in. (7 cm) from the source of heat, until browned on both sides and a little pink in the middle. The time needed will depend on the size and the thickness of the patties. *Serves 6.*

Barbecued Lamb Patties

One of my successful barbecues. As an accompaniment for this dish, I like barley pilaff, fried rice, or hot green noodles tossed with fresh basil, oil and lemon juice.

> 1½–2 lb. (0.75–1 kg) ground lamb
> ½ cup (125 mL) fresh parsley, chopped
> 1 onion, chopped fine
> ½ tsp. (2 mL) basil or sage
> 2 tbsp. (30 mL) prepared horseradish
> ¼ cup (60 mL) chutney or A-1 Sauce
> ¼ cup (60 mL) chili sauce
> 2 tbsp. (30 mL) lemon juice
> ½ tsp. (2 mL) powdered garlic
> 1 tsp. (5 mL) honey or sugar

In a bowl, mix together the lamb, parsley, onion and basil or sage. Shape into patties.

Combine in a bowl the horseradish, chutney or A-1 sauce, chili sauce, lemon juice, garlic, and honey or sugar. Brush half of this mixture over the patties. Barbecue or grill 3 to 4 in. (7.5–10 cm) from source of heat for 8 to 10 minutes. Turn once, top with remaining mustard mixture, and cook for another 5 to 7 minutes. *Makes 6–8 patties.*

Greek Lamb Patties

A true classic of Greek cuisine. Serve them *à la Grecque* — with rice mixed with parsley or mint, and a bowl of plain yogurt.

    1 lb. (0.5 kg) ground lamb
    1 tbsp. (15 mL) vegetable oil
    3 green onions, chopped
    1 tbsp. (15 mL) dried mint leaves
    3 tbsp. (50 mL) chopped parsley
    1½ tsp. (7 mL) salt
    ¼ tsp. (1 mL) pepper
    Juice of ½ a lemon
    ½ lb. (0.25 kg) mushrooms, sliced
    ½ cup (125 mL) yogurt or commercial sour cream

Heat the oil in a frying pan, add the onions and stir over medium heat for a minute. Add lamb and cook over high heat, stirring often, until meat loses its red color.

Crush mint between palms of your hands over the meat, then add the parsley, salt, pepper and lemon juice. Mix well, simmer over low heat 20 minutes, add the mushrooms and simmer 5 minutes over medium heat. Remove from heat, add yogurt or sour cream and stir thoroughly. Heat if necessary, but do not let it boil. *Serves 4.*

Lamb Balls in Avgolemono Sauce

Another Greek specialty. *Avgolemono* means "egg and lemon," the two important finishing ingredients of so many Greek dishes. When possible, replace the water with chicken or lamb stock — it makes a perfect, light and tasty dish, great for summer and spring.

    1 lb. (0.5 kg) ground lamb
    1 onion, grated
    3 tbsp. (50 mL) uncooked rice
    1 tsp. (5 mL) salt
    ¼ tsp. (1 mL) pepper
    ⅛ tsp. (0.5 mL) thyme
    2 tbsp. (30 mL) flour
    3 cups (750 mL) water
    2 eggs
    Juice of ½ a lemon
    1–3 tbsp. (15–50 mL) chopped fresh mint

Knead the lamb, onion, rice, salt, pepper and thyme in a bowl until thoroughly mixed, then shape into small meatballs and set on a plate. Mix flour with ½ cup (125 mL) of water in a saucepan and, when smooth, add the rest of the water, beating well. Cook over medium heat until mixture starts bubbling, then add meatballs one by one. Cook uncovered over low heat 40 minutes, then remove from heat, stirring 3 or 4 times.

In a separate bowl beat eggs slightly, add lemon juice and beat for another minute. While still beating, gradually add a few spoonfuls of the hot meat sauce. Mix well, then pour into meatball sauce. Stir just enough to blend together, but do not let sauce boil. Pour meat balls and sauce into a hot serving dish and sprinkle with fresh mint or parsley. *Serves 4.*

Luncheon Lamb Loaf

Equally good hot or cold. Perfect for sandwiches. When I make it with celery root, I brush the top of the loaf with ¼ cup (60 mL) of chutney, then top it with the onions and bacon slices.

1½ lb. (0.75 kg) ground lamb
2 cups (500 mL) raw carrots or celery root, peeled and grated
1½ cups (375 mL) soft bread cubes
1 egg, beaten
½ cup (125 mL) ketchup
1 onion, chopped fine
1 tsp. (5 mL) salt
¼ tsp. (1 mL) pepper
1½ tsp. (7 mL) thyme or basil
1 tsp. (5 mL) paprika
¼ cup (60 mL) chopped celery leaves
1 small onion
3 to 6 slices bacon

Combine all ingredients in a bowl, except onion and bacon, then mix thoroughly. Press into a well-greased 9 x 5 x 3-in. (22.5 x 12.5 x 7.5 cm) loaf pan. Slice onion, break into rings, and place on top of loaf, gently pressing them into the meat. Top with the bacon slices. Bake 1 hour in a 325°F. (165°C) oven. To serve hot, strain drippings and make a flour-thickened sauce. To serve cold, cover loaf with foil as soon as you remove it from oven. Put something heavy (a can of fruit, a saucepan cover, etc.) on top, and let cool at room temperature; then refrigerate overnight before removing weight. *Serves 6.*

Lamb and Beer Loaf

In 1972 I was doing some films for television in Denmark. At one point, a chef made this loaf for us and gave me the recipe. We enjoyed it cold the next day, while sitting outside on the grass. With Danish black bread and the super unsalted Danish butter, the *Kodrulle lol*, as the chef called this pâté, was terrific. I have been making it ever since.

> 2 lb. (1 kg) ground lamb
> 1 lb. (0.5 kg) uncooked ground ham
> 1½ cups (375 mL) soda cracker crumbs
> 2 eggs, well beaten
> ½ tsp. (2 mL) each salt and pepper
> Beer (Danish, when available)

Ask your butcher to grind together the lamb and the pork. Or use your food processor and grind the meat in 3 separate parts. Place in a large bowl and add the soda cracker crumbs, eggs, salt and pepper. Blend together thoroughly and shape in a loaf or a tube shape. Roll into a piece of cheesecloth or clean cotton, and tie it at both ends. Place in a large saucepan on an inverted saucer or a rack, and add enough beer to cover the loaf. Bring to a boil, cover and simmer over very low heat for 2 hours. Remove from liquid, and set on a platter. Cool and refrigerate at least 12 hours before unwrapping.

I like to serve it thinly sliced, with pickled beets and a potato salad. *Serves* 6.

My Own Bacon Lamb Roll

This recipe is very much a part of my "cooking vocabulary." I make it at least 10 or 12 times a year. I love it hot, with baked potatoes. I love it cold with a crisp spinach salad. I love to take a slice of toasted French bread, spread with good mustard (no butter), and put a slice of this delicious loaf on top. I just love it . . . period.

2 lb. (1 kg) ground lamb
1½ cups (375 mL) soda cracker crumbs
1 large onion, chopped fine or grated
3 eggs, well beaten
⅓ cup (80 mL) heavy cream
1½ tsp. (7 mL) salt
½ tsp. (2 mL) nutmeg
½ tsp. (2 mL) pepper
¼ tsp. (1 mL) thyme
¼ tsp. (1 mL) allspice
½ lb. (0.25 kg) bacon, thinly sliced

Put all the ingredients except the bacon in a bowl and mix thoroughly.

Place a square of wax paper on the table. Arrange the slices of bacon in a row in the middle of it. Shape the meat into a roll as long as the length of the bacon slices, and set on top of the bacon. Lift up one edge of the paper to place one end of the bacon on top of the meat roll, then repeat with the other edge. Shape as firmly as possible, lift with the paper and roll into a baking pan long enough to fit the roll. It is easy to do when using the paper to do the work. (Carefully remove it from the pan before baking.) Bake in a preheated 350°F. (180°C) oven, 1 hour and 15 minutes. Cool and refrigerate, covered. *Serves 6–8.*

Loukanika

Small Greek homemade sausages, so good there never seems to be enough. Serve piping hot, right out of the broiler. I serve mine with sticks of cucumber or fingers of toasted Greek bread.

    1 lb. (0.5 kg) ground lamb
    1 lb. (0.5 kg) ground pork or beef
    2–3 cloves crushed garlic
    1 tsp. (5 mL) each cinnamon and allspice
    1 tsp. (5 mL) pepper
    Grated rind of 1 orange
    15 peppercorns, coarsely cracked
    ½ cup (125 mL) dry red wine

Place all the ingredients in a bowl. Mix thoroughly with your hands, cover and refrigerate for one week, mixing thoroughly once a day. Then shape into 8 to 12-in. (20–30 cm) sausages. Place on a dish, one next to the other. Cover with a cloth. Refrigerate 24 hours.

To serve, cut in 1-in. (2.5 cm) pieces and broil for 2 to 3 minutes. As soon as you take them out of the oven, sprinkle with fresh lemon juice and serve. *Yield: 2–2½ dozen.*

Good Earth Lamb Casserole

Ground lamb, fruits and vegetables are combined to make this interesting one-dish family meal. The addition of wheat germ and sesame seeds gives it the "good earth" appeal.

    1 lb. (0.5 kg) ground lamb
    1 large onion, peeled and sliced
    ¼ cup (60 mL) seedless raisins
    2 apples, cored and chopped
    1 clove garlic, chopped fine
    ⅓ cup (80 mL) fresh parsley, chopped
    1 tsp. (5 mL) salt
    ½ tsp. (2 mL) pepper
    ¼ tsp. (1 mL) dill seeds
    2–3 cups (500–750 mL) shredded cabbage
    ¼ cup (60 mL) wheat germ
    1 tsp. (5 mL) corn starch
    ½ cup (125 mL) chicken broth or water
    3 tbsp. (50 mL) sesame seeds

Crumble the ground lamb in a frying pan over medium heat and cook, stirring often, until meat is lightly browned here and there. Stir in the onion, and keep cooking and stirring until the onion is limp. Add the raisins, apples, garlic, parsley, salt, pepper and dill seeds. Stir well, cover and simmer over low heat about 10 minutes. Stir in the shredded cabbage and wheat germ. Cover and simmer 5 minutes more, stirring once. Mix together the corn starch and chicken broth or water, and add to mixture. Cook, stirring until thick and creamy.

Sprinkle some sesame seeds over each portion when serving. Can be served with butter rice or as a garnish. *Serves 4.*

3

Chops
and Steaks

Two Ways to Pan-Fry Lamb Chops

1. Heat a heavy frying pan just large enough to hold the desired number of chops. Add chops, cover pan, and cook 3 minutes over high heat. Uncover and turn the chops. Cook uncovered for 4 minutes over high heat. The time may vary slightly according to the thickness of the chops. Add salt and pepper to taste just before serving.
2. Melt 1 tbsp. (15 mL) fat or butter (or fat removed from the lamb) in a heavy frying pan. Place the chops in the fat and cook 4 minutes over high heat. Set the heat high enough so that the chops neither simmer nor burn. Turn them, and cook for another 4 minutes. Salt and pepper to taste.

Broiled Lamb Chops à la Grecque

Lemon and lamb are the best of friends, as the Greeks discovered long ago.

> 6 loin or rib lamb chops, 1 in. (2.5 cm) thick
> Juice and grated peel of 1 lemon
> Salt and pepper to taste

Make incisions in the lean part of the chops. Stuff with the lemon peel and sprinkle the chops with the lemon juice. Season to taste and let stand 3 to 4 hours at room temperature.

Place marinated chops on grill of broiler pan, 4 in. (10 cm) from the source of heat. (These may also be pan-fried.) *Serves 4-6.*

Loin Chops Glacé

These pan-broiled chops with their shiny glaze on top are France's gift to lamb connoisseurs. Serve with 1 cup (250 mL) of long grain rice cooked in 1 cup (250 mL) each fresh orange juice and water, and ½ cup (125 mL) finely diced celery.

    4 loin lamb chops, 1-in. (2.5 cm) thick
    3 tbsp. (50 mL) red currant jelly
    Juice of ½ a lemon
    1 tsp. (5 mL) steak sauce
    2 tbsp. (30 mL) hot water

Remove a few pieces of fat from each chop and melt in a cast-iron frying pan. Pan-broil chops in melted fat about 5 minutes per side, over medium heat, turning once only.

Mix together remaining ingredients, pour over cooked chops; cover and simmer over low heat 5 minutes. Turn meat, and cook uncovered until bottoms of chops are glazed. Place in the middle of a hot platter, surround with the "orange" rice, and garnish with bouquets of cool, crisp watercress (when available). *Serves 4.*

English Mixed Grill

An elegant, delicious and easy-to-prepare "brunch." Simply serve with a good chutney, toasted oatmeal bread, and a glass of *cool* port wine. If you're lucky enough to have a garden and spring flowers, you can make-believe you are somewhere in the beautiful English countryside.

4 loin or rib lamb chops
2 lamb kidneys, cut in half (optional)
8 pork sausages
4 small to medium tomatoes, halved
¼ tsp. (2 mL) sugar
2 tbsp. (30 mL) butter
8 large mushrooms (optional)
8 slices bacon

Place the chops on the broiler rack, and set on the broiler pan, 3 in. (7.5 cm) from the source of heat. Broil 10 minutes on one side, turn, sprinkle with salt, pepper and paprika, and broil another 5 minutes. Then place the kidneys, sausages, tomatoes and the mushrooms around the meat, and brush with melted butter. Set the bacon on top of the tomatoes. Return pan to oven and broil 3 to 5 minutes more. *Serves 4.*

Braised Arm Lamb Chops

Arm chops are cut from the shoulder, and contain more bones than other chops. They take longer to cook, as they are at their best "moist cooked," such as in the following recipe. These are economical and very tasty.

4 arm lamb chops, 1-in. (2.5 cm) thick
2 tbsp. (30 mL) butter
2 tbsp. (30 mL) diced lamb fat
3 tbsp. (50 mL) dry sherry or Madeira
½ tsp. (2 mL) paprika
1 small tomato, unpeeled and diced
2 tbsp. (30 mL) flour
1½ cups (375 mL) undiluted canned consommé
1 bay leaf
2 tbsp. (30 mL) dry sherry (optional)

Melt the butter and diced lamb fat in a Dutch oven. Brown the chops quickly over high heat. Pour the dry sherry or Madeira on top. Bring it to a quick boil, and remove from heat. Place the chops on a plate. To the fat remaining in the pan, add the paprika and the diced tomato. Stir a minute or two over medium heat. Add the flour, mix well, add the consommé and the bay leaf. Stir until the mixture comes to a boil. Return the chops to the sauce with any juice accumulated in the plate. Salt and pepper. Cover and simmer over low heat about 30 to 40 minutes or until meat is tender. Serve with potatoes and carrots, boiled, drained and mashed together with a bit of cream and chopped parsley. *Serves 4.*

Teriyaki Lamb Chops

Teriyaki marinade-basting sauce is just super with lamb chops. I like to grill them outdoors over coals in the summer, but I use my oven grill in the winter with equal success. To prepare these, I recommend rib or blade chops for a more economical cut.

> 4 rib or blade chops, 1-in. (2.5 cm) thick
> ¼ cup (60 mL) brown sugar
> 1 tbsp. (15 mL) fresh lemon juice
> Grated rind of 1 lemon
> 1 clove garlic, chopped fine
> ½ tsp. (2 mL) fresh ginger root, grated

Place chops in a shallow baking dish. Combine the remaining ingredients, and pour mixture over the chops; cover and refrigerate 4 to 6 hours. When ready to grill, place chops 4 in. (10 cm) from source of heat, broil 4 to 6 minutes on each side, turning once and basting a few times with the remaining marinade.

Add a green salad and a baked potato, and you have a perfect meal. *Serves 4.*

Italian Lamb Chops

A practical recipe since it is equally good whether using loin, rib or shoulder chops. Rib and loin are cooked the same length of time; for the shoulder chops, 15 minutes is added to the overall cooking period.

6 loin, rib or shoulder lamb chops
1 tbsp. (15 mL) vegetable oil
½ tsp. (2 mL) salt
½ tsp. (2 mL) pepper
½ tsp. (2 mL) basil or oregano
1 garlic clove, crushed
Juice of 1 lemon
½ tsp. (2 mL) French Dijon mustard

Remove excess fat from the chops. Mix together the oil, salt, pepper, basil or oregano and garlic, and roll the chops in the mixture. Use right away or marinate in the liquid for 2 hours at room temperature.

Broil or pan-fry, with or without fat. When broiled, better results are obtained when the chops are marinated.

When ready to serve, set the chops on a hot platter and pour over them the lemon juice mixed with the mustard. *Serves 6.*

Turkish Pan-Fried Lamb Steaks

In Turkey they use a mustard similar to French or German mustard and dark (buckwheat) honey for the glaze. They serve the steaks on a bed of paper-thin slices of peeled cucumber rolled in fresh chopped mint.

2 lamb steaks of your choice, about 1-in. (2.5 cm) thick
1 tsp. (5 mL) prepared mustard
1 tsp. (5 mL) honey
Pinch of thyme

Melt 1 tbsp. (15 mL) of fat trimmed from the steaks in a cast-iron frying pan [or use 1 tbsp. (15 mL) each vegetable oil and butter]. When hot, add the steaks, placed side by side, and cook 4 minutes over medium-high heat. Turn, lower the heat and cook another 4 to 7 minutes, until they are done to your taste.

Five minutes before the end of the cooking period, brush each steak with a mixture of the prepared mustard, honey and thyme. Cover the pan. Turn off the heat and let stand 5 minutes. Uncover, turn each steak and rub into juice in bottom of pan. Serve, pouring a spoonful of the gravy over each steak. *Serves 4.*

Broiled Lamb Steaks

Steak cuts from the leg, broiled or barbecued, are tender and tasty. Serve with a chutney, broiled tomatoes, baked potatoes, and a dry red wine.

4 small lamb steaks, 1 in. (2.5 cm) thick
1 tbsp. (15 mL) vegetable oil
½ tsp. (2 mL) paprika
Salt and pepper to taste
¼ tsp. (1 mL) oregano, basil or rosemary

Place steaks on wax paper. Combine the remaining ingredients and rub generously on both sides of the steaks. Let stand 1 hour at room temperature.

Preheat broiler. Place steaks on broiler rack, set 3 to 4 in. (7.5–10 cm) from the source of heat. For rare, broil 8 minutes, turn, and broil another 1 to 2 minutes. For medium to well done, broil 14 minutes. *Serves 4.*

Baked Lamb Steak Bigarade

A *bigarade* always indicates a meat cooked or flavored with fresh oranges. These lamb steaks are a classic of the French cuisine. Serve with steamed buttered broccoli.

> 2 large lamb steaks, 1 in. (2.5 cm) thick
> 1 tsp. (5 mL) salt
> 2 unpeeled oranges, sliced
> 2 tbsp. (30 mL) brown sugar
> 1 tbsp. (15 mL) orange rind
> ½ tsp. (2 mL) ground ginger
> ¼ tsp. (1 mL) ground cloves
> 1 tsp. (5 mL) dried mint
> ¼ cup (60 mL) melted butter

Place the steaks in a 1½ to 2-in. (4–5 cm) deep baking dish, and sprinkle salt over them to taste. Cover with the orange slices. Mix together the remaining ingredients and pour over the oranges.

Bake 40 minutes in a 325°F. (165°C) oven, basting several times with the juice. *Serves 4.*

Crusty Roasted Rack of Lamb

A favorite of the best restaurants. Prepare the day before, wrap and refrigerate overnight. One hour before roasting, unwrap and place on rack in shallow roasting pan and let stand at room temperature.

    2 racks of lamb (6–7 ribs each)
    2 cups (500 mL) fresh, fine breadcrumbs
    1 cup (250 mL) chopped parsley
    1 tsp. (5 mL) basil or rosemary
    2 cloves garlic, crushed
    2 tsp. (10 mL) salt
    ½ tsp. (2 mL) freshly ground pepper
    1 tsp. (5 mL) paprika
    ½ cup (125 mL) olive or vegetable oil

Trim excess fat from racks if necessary. In a bowl combine the remaining ingredients, toss and stir until thoroughly mixed. Cover top of each rack with half of the mixture over the meaty side. Press well, so it will stay in place. Wrap tightly and refrigerate.

When ready to roast (after unwrapping and letting stand one hour at room temperature), place on rack in shallow roasting pan. Roast 10 to 12 minutes per lb. (0.5 kg) in a 375°F. (190°C) oven. *Serves 6–8.*

Rothschild Roll

The boned 12- to 14-rib loin and the kidneys will have to be ordered ahead of time, as they are not usually available at the meat counter. This is a very spectacular piece to serve at a very special dinner. It was created by the great master chef, Escoffier, around 1909, for Baron Rothschild.

> 1 boned 12- to 14-rib lamb loin
> 4 lamb kidneys
> ¼ cup (60 mL) chutney
> 1 tsp. (5 mL) salt
> ¼ tsp. (1 mL) freshly ground pepper
> ¼ tsp. (1 mL) rosemary
> ¼ cup (60 mL) melted butter
> 8–10 medium potatoes
> Paprika
> ¼ cup (60 mL) brandy or dry port wine

Ask your butcher to bone a 12- to 14-rib loin of lamb. Place in the middle (in a row on top of the meat) the fat-trimmed kidneys, left whole or cut in half. Tie into a long roll with string. Put the meat in a roasting pan, and rub the chutney on the kidneys through the opening between the string. Turn the roll so the opening touches the bottom. Sprinkle the top with the salt, pepper, rosemary or basil, and drip the melted butter over all.

Peel the potatoes and cut each one in thin slices without cutting right through, so that they stay in one piece. Place them around the meat and roll them in the butter at the bottom of the pan. Sprinkle with paprika.

Bake 1¼ hours in a preheated 350°F. (180°C) oven. The potatoes may be turned twice while cooking, so they will brown evenly.

Add the brandy or port to the gravy in the pan, and stir, scraping bottom of pan. Bring just to a boil, and strain into a hot gravy boat. To serve, place the roast on a hot platter and surround with the potatoes. No other garnish is necessary. Slice thinly. *Serves 6.*

Rack of Lamb the French Way

In the true French tradition, a rack is flavored with rosemary, olive oil and lemon rind — but never lemon juice, since Madeira wine is used for the gravy.

> 2–3 lb. (1–1.5 kg) rack of lamb
> Salt and pepper
> ½ tsp. (2 mL) rosemary or basil
> ½ tsp. (2 mL) grated fresh ginger
> Grated rind of 1 lemon
> 3 tbsp. (50 mL) olive or peanut oil
> 2 tbsp. (30 mL) cold water
> 2 tbsp. (30 mL) dry Madeira or sherry

Sprinkle the rack of lamb with salt and pepper, then with the rosemary or basil, grated fresh ginger and grated lemon rind.

Place meat in a roasting pan the same size as the meat. (If the pan is too large, the gravy will dry up.) Pour the olive or peanut oil on top of the lamb. Roast 18 minutes per lb. (0.5 kg) in a preheated 400°F. (200°C) oven.

To make the gravy, remove meat from pan, and add the cold water and dry Madeira or sherry mixed together. Scrape bottom of pan over direct heat to give color to the gravy. Strain or serve as is. *Serves 2–4.*

Japanese Rack of Lamb

This is perhaps the most popular cut when one wishes to serve an elegant dinner for two. Three-star restaurants and hotels serve it to order only, and it is considered a very special dinner. Do not let the first 30-minute cooking period at 400°F. (200°C) worry you — the results are fantastic!

> One small rack of lamb, 1½–2 lb. (0.75–1 kg)
> ½ cup (125 mL) Japanese soy sauce
> ¼ cup (60 mL) Seville orange marmalade
> 1 tsp. (2 mL) grated fresh ginger
> Juice of ½ a lemon

Place rack as is, without adding anything, in a roasting pan, and place pan in a preheated 400°F. (200°C) oven for 30 minutes.

Mix together the soy sauce (whenever possible, use a Japanese type which is far more delicate than the Chinese), the orange marmalade, grated fresh ginger and the lemon juice. Pour this mixture over the rack of lamb after it has been cooking for 30 minutes. Roast for another 20 to 25 minutes, depending on the way you prefer the meat, pink or well done.

To make the gravy, simply add a few spoonfuls of cold water. Stir the mixture. *Serves 2–3.*

4

Shish Kebabs

The history of shish kebabs goes back a long way. We take it for granted that the first time men cooked meat, it certainly was not in a roasting pan in the oven.

In the Orient in feudal times, meat was forbidden to peasants. So they had to find a way of quickly disposing of their poached game and small animals right there in the fields where they were working (since being caught with meat meant severe punishment). They built wood fires — supposedly to brew their tea — and placed on the fire the hoes that they always carried with them. When the hoes were hot, they placed pieces of meat, cut in cubes or strips, on top of them, and cooked them in the fire. Sometimes they cut a branch from a tree and put it through 5 or 6 pieces of meat, and in so doing created the first real shish kebab. Warriors also used their swords in this way to spear meat and cook it over their *bivouac* fires in the battlefield.

The Japanese name for kebab is *sukiyaki*, which is a combination of the words *suki* (meaning hoe) and *yaki* (meaning to broil). The popularity of this means of cooking meat spread far and wide, from the *Shish Kebab* of the Near East, the *Sates* of Indonesia, the *Teriyaki* of Hawaii, the *Shashlyk* of Russia, and the *Sis Kebop* of Turkey. The Greek *Souvlakia* is, to my taste, perhaps the simplest and most ingeniously flavored of all kebabs. But they are all most enjoyable eating.

Greek Souvlakia

Serve the kebabs piping hot, with the dip sauce of yogurt and fresh mint as cool as possible. An exciting experience of hot and cold in one bite.

Double recipe

2 lb. (1 kg) boneless leg of lamb
1 onion, chopped fine
1 tbsp. (15 mL) olive or vegetable oil
2 tbsp. (30 mL) chopped parsley *(use dry parsley flakes)*
(2 tsp. (10 mL) salt *omit*)
½ tsp. (2 mL) freshly ground pepper - *use pepper from shaker*
12–16 bay leaves
2 very firm tomatoes
1 tsp. (5 mL) oregano
1 cup (250 mL) unflavored yogurt
2 tbsp. (30 mL) fresh mint, chopped

marinade

Cut the meat into pieces the size of a large walnut. Place in a bowl with the onion, oil, parsley, salt and pepper. Roll meat in this mixture until well coated. Let stand 1 hour or overnight, covered and refrigerated.

Cut tomatoes into 8 quarters; place 5 or 6 pieces of meat on skewers, alternating with tomatoes and a bay leaf. Pierce tomato pieces through the skin side, so they will not fall off during the broiling.

Broil over charcoal or under oven broiler, 2 in. (5 cm) away from source of heat. Sprinkle each piece with a bit of oregano once during the broiling. They should be done in about 10 minutes for rare, and 15 minutes for medium.

Serve *à la Grecque*, one skewer for each person, on a large paper napkin. Mix the yogurt and fresh mint to use as a dipping sauce, or serve with quartered lime or lemon. *Serves 6–8.*

Turkish Sis Kebop

When it comes to barbecue showmanship, nothing is more spectacular than these delicate shiny "lamb chops" strung on long silver skewers with pieces of fresh corn and squares of green pepper. When I serve these in the summer, I place the cooked *Kebop* on a large slice of toasted and buttered homemade bread, sprinkled generously with minced chives.

> 8 small lamb chops 1½-in. (3.75 cm) thick
> ½ cup (125 mL) milk or light cream
> ¼ cup (60 mL) freshly ground black coffee or dry instant coffee
> 1 tsp. (5 mL) sugar
> 6–8 ears of corn, shucked and cut in three
> 2 green peppers, cut into squares

Place lamb chops side by side in a dish. Mix together the cream, coffee and sugar, and heat until just warm. Stir well and pour over the lamb chops. Cover and marinate 4 to 12 hours, turning them once.

To barbecue or grill, run a skewer through each lamb chop lengthwise, avoiding the round or the blade bone. Place on grill 5 or 6 in. (13–15 cm) away from source of heat. Broil 6 to 8 minutes on each side, turning only once, brushing 3 to 4 times with the remaining coffee marinade.

Remove from heat and alternate on skewers squares of green pepper and pieces of corn (insert lengthwise through the cob — easy to do if you wear gloves and use a slightly twisting motion). Proceed the same for each skewer. If there is any marinade left, use it to brush on the vegetables; return to the grill and broil 4 to 8 minutes more on each side.

To serve, place the point of each skewer on a slice of bread sprinkled with minced chives if you wish to serve them this way, and with a fork use the lamb chop to push the vegetables off the skewer. *Serves 6–8.*

Tehran Shish Kebab

To most Iranians, beef is taboo, so a true Shish Kebab is always cut from the leg or the shoulder of young lamb. They are served piping hot with a bowl of plain rice, a raw egg yolk set in a hole in the middle of the hot rice, and pieces of baked tomato both stirred by each person into the hot rice and eaten with the meat.

> 2 lb. (1 kg) boneless lamb from the leg or shoulder
> ¼ cup (60 mL) olive or vegetable oil
> ¼ cup (60 mL) fresh lemon juice
> 2 cloves minced garlic
> 1 tsp. (5 mL) salt
> ½ tsp. (2 mL) freshly ground pepper
> ½ tsp. (2 mL) barakat or anise seeds

Cut the meat in 1½-in. (3.75 cm) pieces. Mix the remaining ingredients in a bowl. Roll the pieces of lamb in the mixture until they are well coated. Cover and marinate in the refrigerator for 24 hours.

Thread a few squares of the meat on each skewer. Brush each one with a bit of the marinade at the bottom of the bowl. Broil on barbecue or in oven 4-in. (10 cm) away from source of heat, about 15 minutes, or until meat is browned. Serve with the rice, egg yolk and tomato, letting each person stir it together to taste. *Serves 4.*

Indonesian Sates

In Holland, where I lived for a year, I learned to make some super Indonesian dishes, among them *sates,* which is the Far Eastern way of making kebabs. The Indonesians often serve two kebabs with hot rice topped with fresh grated ginger root and buttered dry currants.

2 lb. (1 kg) boneless cubes of lamb
3 onions, peeled and chopped fine
2 cloves garlic, peeled and minced
1 tbsp. (15 mL) coriander seeds, crushed
Salt and pepper to taste
Grated rind of 1 lemon
¼ cup (60 mL) fresh lemon juice
2 tbsp. (30 mL) brown sugar
2 tbsp. (30 mL) soy sauce

In a large bowl, mix the onion, garlic, coriander, salt and pepper. Add lemon rind, juice, brown sugar and soy sauce. Mix thoroughly, and add cubes of lamb. Cover, and let stand 1 to 2 hours at room temperature.

To broil, string 4 to 6 pieces of meat on each skewer. Broil 3 to 4 in. (7.5–10 cm) from source of heat for 8 to 10 minutes, or until golden brown, turning only once. Serve with a bowl of garnished hot rice. *Serves 6.*

Oriental Kebabs

These Kebabs, made all over the Middle East, are so called because of the walnuts used in the recipe, and because the meat is mixed for 5 minutes, giving them a fine texture. A low-cost ground lamb kebab, that can be a tasty barbecue in the summer or an elegant broiled appetizer in the winter. Equally good broiled or barbecued.

    2 lb. (1 kg) ground lamb
    ½ cup (125 mL) walnuts, chopped fine (optional)
    ½ cup (125 mL) fresh parsley or celery leaves, chopped fine
    1 tsp. (5 mL) salt
    ¼ tsp. (1 mL) pepper
    1 clove garlic, chopped fine
    1 tsp. (5 mL) ground cumin

Place in the bowl of an electric mixer the lamb and walnuts. Mix thoroughly with your hands, add the remaining ingredients, and beat 5 minutes in the mixer at medium speed. Cover and refrigerate for 1 hour.

Form into 1-in. (2.5 cm) balls. Place 3 or 4 on each skewer. Broil 3 in. (7.5 cm) from direct heat, or on a barbecue, for 5 minutes or until golden brown. *Serves 6.*

Hawaiian Kabob

When I was a guest at a fabulous barbecue in Hawaii, I learned how to prepare these. The presentation was as spectacular and elegant as the food. The prepared kabobs were spread on a thick bed of sprigs of fresh mint, garnished with tiny sprays of fresh ginger flowers that looked like tiny white orchids. There was a large basket lined around the edges with heads of pineapple cut into four pieces and filled with small, hot loaves of bread that were a cross between an English muffin and a *bap*. And to top it all off, a bowl of fresh pieces of pineapple marinated in rum and covered with pink ice cubes (if you want to do this, color your ice cubes with a dash of red food coloring). The combination of the sizzling kabobs, hot bread and iced pineapple is something to remember.

2–3 lb. (1–1.5 kg) boneless lamb shoulder or leg
    cut into 1-in. (2.5 cm) cubes
1 tbsp. (15 mL) fresh ginger root, grated
1 tsp. (5 mL) dry mustard
2 tsp. (10 mL) sugar
½ cup (125 mL) Japanese soy sauce *or* Teriyaki sauce
¼ cup (60 mL) vegetable oil
2–3 cloves garlic, minced
½ cup (125 mL) fresh crushed pineapple

Place pieces of peeled fresh pineapple in a blender or food processor, and process until pineapple is a mush.

Combine all the ingredients, except the lamb, in a bowl. When well mixed, add the lamb cubes and stir until well coated with the marinade. Cover and refrigerate 24 to 48 hours. Then arrange lamb on skewers allowing a little space between every two cubes, so it will cook more evenly. Barbecue or broil 3 to 5 in. (7.5–12.5 cm) from source of heat, about 20 to 30 minutes, turning often. If there is any marinade left, brush on meat while cooking. *Serves 6.*

Caucasian Shashlyk

In Russia, there are many ways to prepare kebabs, and although they are all more or less the same, the shashlyk from the Caucasus region is recognized as the best. They are always served with a platter of whole tomatoes, quartered lemons and bunches of scallions or green onions with at least 3 in. (7.5 cm) of green left on them, the part the Russians consider the best of the onion.

    1 large onion, peeled and grated
    1 tbsp. (15 mL) fresh lemon juice
    2 tbsp. (30 mL) olive or vegetable oil
    1 tsp. (5 mL) salt
    1 tsp. (5 mL) paprika
    ½ tsp. (2 mL) crushed black peppercorn
    2 lb. (1 kg) boneless leg or shoulder of lamb,
        cut into 1-in. (2.5 cm) cubes

Mix together in a bowl, the onion, lemon juice, oil, salt, paprika and crushed peppercorns. Stir the meat into the mixture; cover and marinate at room temperature for 2 to 4 hours, stirring meat around 3 or 4 times.

String the cubes of lamb on skewers. Broil 4 to 5 in. (10–12.5 cm) from source of heat, turning once or twice, for 10 to 15 minutes. Serve piping hot. *Serves 4–6.*

Mixed Grill Kebabs

Another elegant summer fare done on the grill or barbecue, topped with fresh mint (or basil) butter. Perfect with a light red wine and crisp hot bread.

        6 lamb kidneys
        6 small rib lamb chops
        6 slices bacon
        18 cherry tomatoes
        12 whole small mushrooms
        6 small sausages
        1 tsp. (5 mL) salt
        ½ tsp. (2 mL) pepper
        1 tsp. (5 mL) ground cumin

Split the kidneys lengthwise, but do not separate them. (If they are difficult to find in quantity, you could use a half per skewer instead of a whole one.) Wrap each kidney with a strip of bacon. Thread each of the 6 skewers with 3 cherry tomatoes, 2 whole mushrooms, 1 small sausage, 1 small lamb chop, and bacon-wrapped kidney. Stir together the salt, pepper and cumin, and sprinkle evenly on the meat; then brush with melted butter. Arrange the skewers over a broiler pan, or place on a barbecue, about 4 in. (10 cm) from the source of heat and broil 10 to 12 minutes, turning them twice and brushing them with butter each time. Serve on very hot plate with a ball of mint (or basil) butter melting on each.

To make the butter, crush 1 small clove of garlic, and add it to ¾ cup (180 mL) soft butter, along with 1 tbsp. (15 mL) finely-chopped fresh mint or basil. Mix together, and add a little salt and pepper, and stir in the juice of ½ a lemon. Chill the butter until it is firm enough to shape into 6 to 8 small balls. Keep refrigerated until ready to serve. *Serves 6.*

5 Leg of Lamb

My Favorite Roast Leg of Lamb

When lamb is cooked in this manner, "pink" or medium-rare, it is perfect even when you serve it cold, in thin slices. The gravy made with dry Madeira wine gives it a very special taste. [Fresh ginger is available at Oriental food stores; but if you cannot get it, you can replace it with 1½ tsp. (7 mL) powdered ginger.]

        1 leg of lamb, 4–6 lb. (2–3 kg)
        1 clove garlic, crushed
        2 tsp. (10 mL) fresh grated ginger
        1 tsp. (5 mL) salt
        ¼ tsp. (1 mL) pepper
        1 tsp. (5 mL) paprika
        2 tbsp. (30 mL) vegetable oil
        Juice and rind of 1 lemon

Place meat on platter. Make a paste with the remaining ingredients, and spread all over the leg of lamb. Cover with waxed paper, and let stand at room temperature for 2 to 4 hours.

To cook, remove the paper and place meat in shallow roasting pan. Roast uncovered 10 minutes in an oven which has been preheated to 500°F. (260°C). Then reduce heat to 325°F. (165°C), and roast about 12–15 minutes per lb. (0.5 kg).

To make the gravy, remove leg to hot platter. Place roasting pan over direct heat. Pour 1 can undiluted consommé over the drippings, and bring to a fast rolling boil, stirring and scraping the pan to make sure you get the browned bits on the bottom. For a variation, at this point you can add 2–3 tbsp. (30–50 mL) dry Madeira or port wine. Strain into a hot gravy bowl.

Serve the lamb on very hot plates, a must for all lamb dishes; this prevents the fat from hardening. *Serves 6–8.*

English Roast Leg of Lamb

I am not usually very partial to serving mint with lamb; but this way of roasting a leg of lamb makes the meat especially moist and tasty, whether it is served hot or at room temperature.

    1 leg of lamb, 4½–5½ lb. (2–2.5 kg)
    1 tsp. (5 mL) freshly ground pepper
    1 tsp. (5 mL) ground ginger
    2 tsp. (10 mL) rosemary
    4 tbsp. (60 mL) chopped fresh mint *or*
      2 tbsp. (30 mL) dried mint

Preheat oven to 500°F. (260°C). Make 6 to 8 incisions in the meat with a pointed knife, fill each one with some of the seasoning mixture, and coat the surface of the meat with the remaining mixture.

Place leg, fat side up, on a rack in roasting pan and roast it uncovered in the middle of the preheated oven for 20 minutes. Then, reduce the heat to 375°F. (190°C) and roast for another 30–45 minutes, or 20 minutes per lb. (0.5 kg) for medium. Let stand 15 minutes at room temperature before serving. Serve with **Escoffier Mint Sauce.** *Serves 6–8.*

Escoffier Mint Sauce

Combine ¼ cup (60 mL) water with 3 tbsp. (50 mL) brown sugar, and bring to boil over high heat, stirring until sugar is dissolved. Remove from the heat and stir in ¼–⅓ cup (60–80 mL) finely chopped fresh mint and ½ cup (125 mL) red wine or malt vinegar. Stir well, cover and let stand 2–4 hours before using. *Yield: 1 cup (250 mL).*

Scottish Leg of Lamb

I have never seen anyone but the Scots baste a lamb roast with bacon fat (even fatty lamb gets this treatment). It makes the skin crisp and crunchy, without any taste of bacon. The combination of rosemary and allspice is also intriguing and quite different in flavor from other recipes for roasted leg of lamb.

    1 leg of lamb, 4–5 lb. (1.81–2.27 kg)
    1 tbsp. (15 mL) salt
    1 tsp. (5 mL) freshly ground pepper
    1 tsp. (5 mL) rosemary or basil
    ½ tsp. (2 mL) allspice
    1 tsp. (5 mL) sugar
    ¼ cup (60 mL) hot bacon fat

Rub the leg of lamb with a mixture of the salt, pepper, rosemary, allspice and sugar, and place in dripping pan. Cover with wax paper and let stand 1 hour at room temperature.

Pour the hot bacon fat on top, and place uncovered in a 375°F. (190°C) oven 25 to 30 minutes per lb. (0.5 kg). When done, place on hot serving dish, and let stand 20 minutes in warm place or on hot tray before carving. Make gravy clear or creamy, as you prefer. *Serves 6–8.*

Curried Leg of Lamb

Sensational when you are looking for something different — and it has its own built-in vegetables, so it's a meal in itself.

    1 leg of lamb, 4–6 lb. (2–3 kg)
    1 clove garlic, slivered
    1 tbsp. (15 mL) rosemary
    1 tsp. (5 mL) salt
    ½ tsp. (2 mL) pepper
    1 tbsp. (15 mL) curry powder
    1 cup (250 mL) water
    1 cup (250 mL) hard cider or dry white wine
    6 medium whole carrots
    6 stalks of celery, cut in 2-in. (5 cm) pieces
    8–10 small whole potatoes
    10 small whole onions

Preheat oven to 500°F. !(260°C). Place lamb on a rack which is smaller than the roasting pan. Cut 5 to 6 pockets in the meat with a small pointed knife, and insert in each one a small piece of garlic and a good pinch of rosemary. Sprinkle the roast with a mixture of salt, pepper and curry powder. Pour the water and the cider or wine in the bottom of the roasting pan, and place the vegetables around the meat in the bottom of the pan. Roast 15 minutes at 500°F. (260°C). Lower heat to 350°F. (180°C) and cook medium-rare, or 12 to 15 minutes per lb. (0.5 kg). Turn and baste vegetables 3 or 4 times during the cooking period. *Serves 6–8*.

Butterfly Leg of Lamb

As easy as a chop or steak, this can be broiled in the oven or barbecued over charcoal.

For gravy, heat together ½ cup (125 mL) butter, the juice and rind of 1 lemon, 2 tbsp. (30 mL) freshly chopped mint, and 2 tbsp. (30 mL) minced chives or green onions.

> 1 leg of lamb, 4–6 lb. (2–3 kg)
> 2 tsp. (10 mL) salt
> 1 tsp. (5 mL) freshly ground pepper
> 1 clove garlic, finely chopped
> ½ tsp. (2 mL) thyme
> ½ tsp. (2 mL) oregano
> 3 tbsp. (50 mL) fresh lemon juice
> ½ cup (125 mL) dry red wine
> ½ cup (125 mL) vegetable oil
> 1 bay leaf

Ask the butcher to bone the leg of lamb, leaving it in one piece — not rolled. Place the meat in a large flat glass container. Sprinkle with the salt and pepper, and rub the garlic into the meat. Sprinkle with the remaining ingredients and cover with waxed paper or foil. Refrigerate 24 hours; during that time, turn the meat 3 or 4 times in the marinade mixture.

When ready to cook, remove the meat from the marinade. Dry with paper toweling and reserve marinade left in dish. The meat is now ready to broil or barbecue over charcoal; cook 10 to 15 minutes per lb. (0.5 kg), turning 3 or 4 times. *Serves 6.*

Honey-Glazed Roast Leg of Lamb

Lamb takes to glazes and sauces as well as ham does, so don't hesitate to use your own favorite ham glazes for lamb as well.

    1 leg of lamb, 4–6 lb. (2–3 kg)
    1 tsp. (5 mL) basil
    1 tsp. (5 mL) salt
    ¼ tsp. (1 mL) pepper
    ¼ cup (60 mL) Dijon or German mustard
    ¼ cup (60 mL) honey
    2 tbsp. (30 mL) soft butter

Rub the leg of lamb with the basil, salt and pepper. Place on rack in roasting pan. Roast in a preheated 325°F. (165°C) oven 20 to 30 minutes per lb. (0.5 kg).

Mix together the mustard, honey and soft butter, and spread on the meat about 20 minutes before it is done. Raise the heat to 400°F. (200°C) and continue to roast the meat until it is nicely glazed, basting 3 to 4 times. Make the gravy the same way as for **My Favorite Roast Leg of Lamb,** using 1 cup (250 mL) ginger ale or ginger beer instead of consommé. *Serves 6–8.*

Swedish Leg of Lamb

For an authentic Swedish touch, serve this with buttered green peas, sprinkled with fresh mint, potatoes browned around the roast, and cool currant jelly to which is added the rind of an orange. Enjoy with a dry red wine.

> 1 leg of lamb, 4–6 lb. (2–3 kg)
> 1 tsp. (5 mL) salt
> ½ tsp. (2 mL) pepper
> ½ tsp. (2 mL) oregano or dill
> 4 tbsp. (60 mL) bacon fat
> 1 medium onion, thinly sliced
> ⅓ cup (80 mL) black or red currant jelly

Place the leg of lamb in a roasting pan. Rub top with salt, pepper, oregano or dill, and let stand 1 hour. Place onion slices on top, and pour bacon fat over them.

Place uncovered in a preheated 350°F. (180°C) oven, and roast medium-rare, or 12 to 15 minutes per lb. (0.5 kg). After the first 20 minutes' cooking time, spoon the currant jelly on top of the roast, and add 1 cup (250 mL) hot water. Make gravy from pan drippings. *Serves 6–8.*

6   *Shoulder*

Lancashire Hot Pot

This is a version of the very old English "Hot Pot" made world-famous through early Shakespearean theater. This and another dish called High Pie were served during the plays. The pot is made of earthenware, about 6 in. (15 cm) deep, and the cooking is done in the oven, with the pot covered. This recipe makes an interesting cold weather buffet casserole.

    6 shoulder lamb chops, 1-in. (2.5 cm) thick
    1 tbsp. (15 mL) butter or bacon fat
    6 medium potatoes
    1 tsp. (5 mL) salt
    ¼ tsp. (1 mL) pepper
    2 bay leaves
    ½ tsp. (2 mL) sage
    4 lamb kidneys (optional)
    ½ lb. (0.25 kg) fresh mushrooms
    3 onions, thinly sliced
    2 cups (500 mL) water or consommé

Coat the bottom and sides of the casserole with all of the butter or bacon fat. Peel and slice the potatoes, and spread ⅓ of them in the bottom of the dish. Top with 3 of the lamb chops, placing them side by side.

Blend together the salt, pepper, crumbled bay leaves and sage, and sprinkle the chops with half of this mixture. When using kidneys, remove their fat, and cut into 4 to 6 slices. Place half of them over the chops, topped by half the sliced mushrooms and onions. Repeat these layers, starting again with the potatoes.

Add the water or consommé. Cover and bake in a preheated 325°F. (165°C) oven for 1½ hours. Uncover and cook another 30–40 minutes, or until top is browned. Sprinkle top with an equal mixture of fresh parsley and fresh mint, chopped together; or use 3 green onions and ⅓ cup (80 mL) celery leaves. *Serves 6–8.*

Lamb-in-the-Basket Hot Pot

This is a specialty of Cumberland, England, where it is usually made with the lamb's neck cut into chops. It's a perfect stew-in-a-casserole for a cold winter night.

2½-3 lb. (5–6 kg) lamb-in-the-basket or cubed shoulder
2 tbsp. (30 mL) drippings or butter
2 onions, finely chopped
½ tsp. (2 mL) thyme
4 tomatoes, peeled and chopped, or a 19 oz. (562 mL) can
    tomatoes
1 tsp. (5 mL) honey or sugar
6 potatoes, peeled or diced
Salt and pepper to taste
½ cup (125 mL) canned consommé or water
Chopped parsley to taste

Cut the lamb in equal pieces and remove excess fat. Brown all the pieces in the drippings or butter over high heat. Add the onions, and stir a few minutes, then pour into a casserole. Sprinkle with the thyme, top with chopped or canned tomatoes; pour honey or sugar on top.

Place the potatoes on top of this, sprinkle with salt and pepper, and add the consommé or water. Cover and bake at 350° F. (175° C) for 1½ hours. Sprinkle generously with parsley and serve with a steak sauce. *Serves 6.*

English Aligot of Lamb

The name Aligot comes from the French *haricots* (dry beans) which the people of Brittany always serve with their roasted or stewed lamb. This diced lamb cooked with navy beans reheats well and keeps for 2–3 months in the freezer. A good casserole to take for a weekend of skiing at the cottage.

> 2–3 lb. (1–1.5 kg) lamb shoulder or "lamb-in-the-basket"
> 1 lb. (0.5 kg) (500 g) navy beans
> 1 onions, stuck with 2 cloves
> 2 bay leaves
> 3 garlic cloves, peeled
> ½ cup (125 mL) flour
> 1 tsp. (5 mL) paprika and sugar
> 1 tbsp. (15 mL) salt
> ½ tsp. (2 mL) pepper
> 6 tbsp. (90 mL) vegetable oil
> 3 leeks or 3 large onions, thinly sliced
> Canned consommé
> Dry red or port wine

Soak beans overnight in enough cold water to cover. Drain, place in saucepan with the onion, bay leaf and 1 garlic clove. Add a little more hot water than needed to cover the beans. Bring to a fast rolling boil, then cover and simmer gently 1½–2 hours, or until beans are tender. Salt to taste. (Salting before this causes some beans to remain hard.)

Cut lamb into individual pieces, and discard excess fat. Stir flour together with paprika, sugar, salt and pepper. Roll lamb pieces in mixture. Then, without crowding pan, brown all over in oil over high heat. Remove browned meat, reduce heat, and add remaining garlic (chopped fine) and leeks or onions. Stir 3–4 minutes.

Put meat back in pan and stir well. Add just enough diluted consommé and wine to cover meat. Bring to a boil, cover and simmer 1–1½ hours or until meat is tender.

Combine lamb and its cooking liquid with drained cooked beans in a medium-size casserole. Bake uncovered in a 350°F. (180°C) oven 30 to 50 minutes, basting from time to time with hot water or a little red wine. When it's moist and mellow in flavor and the beans are soft, it's ready. If you freeze the cooked casserole, thaw it out, then reheat it in a 300°F. (150°C) oven for about 1 hour before serving. *Serves 8.*

Loin Chops Glacé
These are the most elegant of all chops; lightly sprinkled with fresh grated lemon rind
before broiling, they are extra super.

Pan-Fried Lamb Kidneys
Lamb kidneys grilled in a Chinese cast-iron pan, with just a touch of chutney and bacon fat —very special.

French Lamb Navarin

This dish is synonymous with spring in France. It is a stew with a difference. Serve with noodles tossed with the first garden chives or parsley.

2–4 lb. (1–2 kg) shoulder of lamb, cut in 1-in. (2.5 cm) cubes
1 tsp. (5 mL) salt
½ tsp. (2 mL) pepper
¼ tsp. (1 mL) nutmeg
4 tbsp. (60 mL) butter or fat
2 large onions, finely chopped
3 tbsp. (50 mL) all-purpose flour
2 cups (500 mL) water
½ cup (125 mL) carrots, diced
½ cup (125 mL) turnips, diced
½–1 cup (125–250 mL) potatoes, diced

Mix together the salt, pepper and nutmeg, and roll the lamb in this mixture. Brown over medium heat in the butter or fat. Add the onions and continue cooking for 1 minute. Add the flour and water and, stirring constantly, bring to a boil. Cover and simmer for 1½ hours, then add the vegetables and simmer for another 1½ hours. *Serves 4–5.*

Lamb and Barley Casserole

Barley is the grain with the perfect texture to combine with lamb. Flavored with orange and rosemary, this makes a true gourmet party dish, yet costs little and is quickly prepared.

2–3 lb. (1–1.5 kg) lamb shoulder
2 tbsp. (30 mL) butter or vegetable oil
2 onions, chopped
1 cup (250 mL) pearl barley
2 unpeeled oranges, thinly sliced
¼ tsp. (1 mL) rosemary
Juice of ½ a lemon
3 cups (750 mL) diluted canned consommé, or 3 cups (750 mL)
    water or lamb broth
Salt and pepper to taste

Cut the lamb into individual pieces. Brown with the onions in butter or oil. Place in a casserole and add the rest of the ingredients. Cover and cook at 300°F. (150°C) for 1½–2 hours, or until meat is tender. Remove from oven, and let stand 20 minutes before serving. *Serves 6.*

Marta's Roasted Shoulder of Lamb

My long-time friend Marta is Finnish, and she has a real flair for combining simple ingredients in a way that gives an unusual and always tasty end result.

2–3 lb. (1–1.5 kg) shoulder of lamb
1 large clove of garlic, coarsely chopped
1 large clove of garlic, unpeeled
2 slices bacon, diced
6–8 medium potatoes, peeled and sliced
2 large onions, sliced
Salt and pepper, and basil or fresh dill, to taste
1 cup (250 mL) lamb or chicken broth

Make small cuts here and there in the meat, and insert pieces of garlic. Rub the roasting pan with the second clove of garlic from which a slice has been cut off. Discard. Place lamb in roasting pan, rub top lightly with salt and pepper, and top with diced bacon. Make alternate layers of onions and potatoes around the roast, sprinkling each layer lightly with salt and pepper, and basil or fresh dill. Pour lamb or chicken broth carefully over the vegetables. Roast uncovered in a preheated 350°F. (180°C.) oven, 1¾ to 2 hours or until meat is tender and golden brown.

Serve piping hot with applesauce or cramberry or red currant jelly. *Serves 6–8.*

French Pot Roasted Shoulder

Use either a boned and rolled shoulder, or an unboned type. Serve with parsleyed rice mixed with buttered green peas.

> 1 lamb shoulder, 3–4 lb. (1.5–2 kg)
> ½ tsp. (2 mL) pepper
> 1 tsp. (5 mL) salt
> ½ tsp. (2 mL) paprika
> ¼ tsp. (1 mL) nutmeg
> ½ tsp. (2 mL) sugar
> 3 tbsp. (50 mL) melted margarine or vegetable oil
> 2 onions, sliced

Mix together the salt, pepper, paprika, nutmeg and sugar. Coat the meat, and brown in a skillet over medium heat, turning until it has a golden brown color all over, then add the onions, stir in the fat for a few seconds. Cover and cook 1½ to 2 hours over medium-low heat, or until meat is tender.

To make the gravy, remove lamb, bring drippings to a boil over high heat, until it browns and thickens, stirring constantly. *Serves 6.*

Moroccan Tajin

Lamb is a meat of many moods, as we can see in this braised lamb dish. It is much more than *just* a lamb stew. Try it for its unusual, subtle flavor.

2½ lb. (1.25 kg) lamb shoulder, cut in 1-in. (2.5 cm) cubes
¼ cup (60 mL) olive or vegetable oil
1 clove garlic, finely chopped
1 onion, chopped
2 tsp. (10 mL) salt
½ tsp. (2 mL) freshly ground pepper
1 bay leaf
1 whole clove
3 tbsp. (50 mL) chopped parsley
1 tsp. (5 mL) ground ginger
Pinch of saffron (optional)
2 large tomatoes, chopped
½ cup (125 mL) water
2 large onions, cut in eighths
1 cup (250 mL) seedless raisins
1 tbsp. (15 mL) butter
⅓ cup (80 mL) blanched almonds
3–4 hard-cooked eggs
2 lemons, cut in wedges

Heat the oil in a deep, heavy pan. Add the meat, garlic and chopped onion. Stir the mixture over high heat, until meat has lost its red color, stirring often.

Add the salt, pepper, bay leaf, clove, parsley, ginger, saffron and tomatoes. Stir again over high heat for 3 to 4 minutes. Add the water. Cover and simmer over low heat, about 1¼ hours or until lamb is tender. Stir once or twice.

Meanwhile, sauté the chopped onions in a spoonful or two of oil until golden brown. Soak raisins in warm water for half an hour and drain. Brown the almonds in the butter. Then add it all to the cooked meat. Place in a preheated 400°F. (200°C) oven for 15 minutes. To serve, place on a large platter, and top with the boiled white or sweet potatoes rolled in parsley, or toasted bread. *Serves 6–8*.

Arabic Lamb Shoulder Madîra

If you are in an African country and order a Lamb Madîra, what you'll get is a lamb stew such as this one.

1½ lb. (0.75 kg) lamb shoulder, cut in 2-in. (5 cm) pieces
¼ cup (60 mL) fat removed from meat, diced (optional)
½ tsp. (2 mL) salt
4½ cups (1.2 L) cold water
3 leeks
4 medium onions, sliced
½ tsp. (2 mL) each of powdered cinnamon, cumin and coriander
½ tsp. (2 mL) salt
1 lemon, unpeeled, thinly sliced
½ tsp. (2 mL) salt
⅓ cup (80 mL) fresh mint or parsley, chopped
2–3 potatoes, peeled and diced
1 cup (250 mL) yogurt (optional)
1 tbsp. (15 mL) fresh mint (optional)

Place in a saucepan the meat and fat; add salt and 3 cups (750 mL) of the cold water. Bring to a fast rolling boil over high heat. Pour into a colander and rinse meat thoroughly under cold running water. Wash saucepan.

Return meat to saucepan with the remaining 1½ cups (375 mL) of cold water. Clean and cut the leeks in 1-in. (2.5 cm) lengths (the white and much of the green), and add to lamb with the onions, cinnamon, cumin, coriander and salt. Bring to a boil, cover and simmer over low heat until the meat is tender, which should take from 1 to 1½ hours.

Meanwhile, place lemon slices on a large plate, sprinkle with the salt, and top with the fresh mint or parsley. Let stand 1 to 1½ hours. When the meat is cooked, remove from stock and beat stock containing the onions and leeks with an electric mixer or wire whisk to thicken it. Put the meat back into the creamy sauce and add the lemon slices. Mix well and simmer 15 minutes. Cool and refrigerate 12 hours. To serve, warm up on low heat and add the diced potatoes; simmer until potatoes are tender, about 20 minutes.

If you like, serve with a bowl of cold yogurt stirred with a few spoonfuls of chopped fresh mint. *Serves 6.*

Texan Lamb Stew

Serve the Texan way, with red beans, or with a dish of meatless chili and a green salad.

  3–4 lb. (1.5–2 kg) lamb shoulder, cut in 2-in. (5 cm) cubes
  ½ cup (125 mL) flour
  1 tsp. (5 mL) salt
  ½ tsp. (2 mL) pepper
  ½ tsp. (2 mL) thyme
  3 tbsp. (50 mL) vegetable oil
  1 cup (250 mL) canned consommé, undiluted
  1 cup (250 mL) celery, cut in 1-in. (2.5 cm) pieces
  2 medium onions, chopped
  1 green pepper, diced
  1 large orange, peeled and sliced
  1 apple, peeled and quartered
  ¼ –½ cup (60–125 mL) brandy or rye (optional)

Mix together flour, salt, pepper and thyme, and coat meat pieces all over with mixture.

Heat oil in cast-iron saucepan or Dutch oven, and add meat, a few pieces at a time. Brown over high heat, remove from pan as they become browned on all sides. Then add consommé and all the remaining ingredients except the brandy or rye. Bring to a full rolling boil, and add the meat. Cover and simmer over low heat, 1½ to 1¾ hours, stirring a few times, or until meat is tender. Add the brandy or rye. Stir well, then let stand 20 minutes covered. *Serves 6–8*.

Hawaiian Lamb Shoulder

In this recipe do not worry about the use of 4 garlic cloves; the way they are used actually gives just a delicate garlic flavor to the meat. The finished roast should have a deep brown glaze.

> 1 rolled or cushion shoulder of lamb, about 3½ lb. (1.6 kg)
> 4 garlic cloves, crushed or finely chopped
> ½ cup (125 mL) boiling water
> ⅓ cup (80 mL) honey
> 1 cup (250 mL) Japanese soy sauce
> Juice of 1 orange

In a large bowl, mix the garlic, boiling water, honey and soy sauce. Place the meat in the mixture and roll all around until well coated. Cover and refrigerate for 24 hours, turning the meat 3 or 4 times during this period.

To roast, remove the meat from the marinating mixture and place it directly in the roasting pan. Pour ½ cup (125 mL) of the marinating mixture on top. Roast 20 to 25 minutes per lb. (0.5 kg) in a 350°F. (180°C) oven for medium-rare.

When the meat is cooked, skim off most of the fat and add the orange juice to the drippings. Boil for a few seconds while scraping the bottom of the pan. Serve with fried or curried rice and blanched cauliflower. *Serves 6–8*.

Poached Lamb Shoulder

1 rolled, boned lamb shoulder, 2–3 lb. (1–1.5 kg)
6 tbsp. (90 mL) butter
2 cloves garlic, crushed
1 tbsp. (15 mL) flour
1½ tsp. (7 mL) salt
¼ tsp. (1 mL) pepper
1 tbsp. (15 mL) lemon juice
1 cup (250 mL) currant or mint jelly

Cream together butter, crushed garlic, flour, salt, pepper and lemon juice. Spread this over lamb shoulder, and put roast on a big piece of foil with bones alongside. Draw edges of the foil together, and fold up, leaving room for juice that will collect during baking. Refrigerate 4–6 hours. Cook in 375°F. (190°C) oven, 40 minutes per lb. (0.5 kg). Fifteen minutes before the end of the cooking period, remove lamb from foil, place on heat-proof platter or in shallow baking pan. Discard bones and pour juice into saucepan.

Melt currant or mint jelly over low heat, stirring all the time. Remove strings from roast. Make deep slashes all over roast, and pour melted jelly over lamb and into slashes. Return to oven for about 10 minutes more to glaze. *Serves* 6.

Baked Shoulder Chops

In Southern Italy, they wrap each serving of this in wet parchment, but in Canada you have your choice of see-through roasting film or aluminum foil. Either way, the tasty meat will fall right off the bone.

> 4 shoulder lamb chops, 1½-in. (3.75 cm) thick
> 1 peeled grapefruit, thickly sliced
> 4 onion slices, ¼-in. (0.65 cm) thick
> 4 tbsp. (60 mL) honey
> Salt and pepper to taste

Sprinkle each chop with salt and pepper, and place on a square of roasting film or foil and top with a grapefruit slice, covered with a slice of onion, then 1 tbsp. (15 mL) of honey.

Wrap each chop, and set in a baking dish and bake in a 350°F. (180°C) oven 1½ hours. *Serves 4.*

Curried Shoulder Lamb Chops

These reheat beautifully. After cooking, cool and refrigerate, then reheat, covered, in a 350°F. (180°C) oven until bubbling. Serve with boiled rice.

> 8 shoulder lamb chops, 1-in. (2.5 cm) thick
> 2 tbsp. (30 mL) butter
> 1 clove garlic, crushed
> ½ tsp. (2 mL) ground ginger
> 1 large onion, sliced
> 1 tsp. (5 mL) turmeric
> 1 tbsp. (15 mL) curry powder
> 2 tbsp. (30 mL) flour
> 1 cup (250 mL) dry red wine
> 1 cup (250 mL) water
> 1 large apple, sliced and cored
> ½ cup (125 mL) seedless raisins

Melt butter, brown chops or pieces of lamb on both sides over high heat, then remove from frying pan. To the fat remaining in the pan, add the garlic, ginger and onion, and stir over high heat until onions are soft. Add the turmeric and curry powder, and stir until well blended. Add the flour, mix well and add the wine, water, apple slices and raisins. Bring to a boil, while stirring, Lower heat and simer, uncovered, about 1 hour or until meat is tender. *Serves 6.*

Braised Cubes of Lamb

Not a stew, nor a roast — simply cubes of lamb shoulder or boned breast, simmered in its own juices. Our family likes it served with boiled rice, stirred in with lots of fresh, chopped parsley, and no butter. We pour spoonfuls of the thick rich gravy over the rice on each plate.

2 lb. (1 kg) boneless lamb cut into cubes
2 tbsp. (3 mL) bacon fat or vegetable oil
1 tsp. (5 mL) cider or wine vinegar
1 tsp. (5 mL) suet
½ tsp. (2 mL) dry mustard
1 large clove garlic, chopped
½ tsp. (2 mL) rosemary or basil
1 tbsp. (15 mL) Japanese soy sauce
1 tbsp. (15 mL) hot water

Heat the bacon fat in a heavy metal saucepan. Add the cubes of lamb and brown all over on high heat. Stir together the dry mustard and vinegar, and add it to the remaining ingredients. Stir well, and pour over the meat. Stir the mixture for a minute, cover and simmer over low heat for about 1–1½ hours. Stir once during the cooking period. The meat will make its own juices. Easy to reheat. *Serves 4.*

Walnut Stuffing for Lamb

People in the Caucasus region of Russia are very fond of nuts, oranges and dried fruits mixed into basic stuffing. This recipe is an interesting one to use to stuff a shoulder or a boned breast of lamb, turning an economical cut into an elegant roast.

1 cup (250 mL) dried apricots or prunes
2 cups (500 mL) hot tea
2 cups (500 mL) coarse bread crumbs
¼ cup (60 mL) chopped parsley
½ cup (125 mL) walnuts, coarsely chopped
Grated rind of 1 lemon or lime
1 egg
2 tbsp. (30 mL) cream or vodka
1 tsp. (5 mL) salt
½ tsp. (2 mL) pepper

Cover the apricots or prunes with hot tea. Soak 6–12 hours; remove pits when using prunes. Drain and cut fruit into small pieces with scissors.

Place prepared fruit in a bowl, and add remaining ingredients thoroughly mixed together. Use to stuff the roast of your choice. Roll and tie roast, and cook in a 325°F. (165°C) oven for 30 minutes per lb. (0.5 kg) for either type of roast. *Serves 6.*

7

Fore Shanks and Neck

These two cuts are often ignored, yet they are so tasty, meaty and low-priced that I always wonder why they are most often turned into ground lamb. I assure you that once you have learned to prepare them, you will understand my taste for them.

Both make perfect barbecued meat. They are equally good either braised in the oven or on top of the stove.

If you do not find them in your store, ask your butcher to keep the fore shanks whole. They are about 4–6 in. (8–12 cm) long, and they make a portion just right for one. Have the neck sliced 1–1½ in. (2–3.5 cm) thick; one or two per person will be sufficient. The meat called for in any of the following recipes can be replaced by an equal amount of shoulder lamb chops or "lamb-in-a-basket," an assortment of shoulder and neck pieces.

Lamb Shanks à la Bretonne

This is one of my most successful buffet casseroles. It tastes even better reheated, so make it 2–3 days ahead of time.

> 3–4 lamb fore shanks, 1 lb. (0.5 kg) each, or larger
>   if you can get them
> 1 cup (250 mL) dried green flageolet beans,
>   or small dried lima beans
> 1 tsp. (5 mL) salt
> 4 tbsp. (60 mL) chopped green onions
> 1 tbsp. (15 mL) olive oil or pan fat
> 2 cups (500 mL) chopped stewed tomatoes, fresh or canned
> 1 cup (250 mL) red wine
> 2 tsp. (10 mL) grated lemon rind
> 1 tsp. (5 mL) crumbled dried oregano
> Freshly ground black pepper
> Chopped parsley

Start this dish a day ahead of time. If you don't have a covered casserole or braising pan large enough [3 quarts (3 L) at least] to hold the fore shanks whole, ask your butcher to cut them in two. Place shanks (and only shanks) in casserole, cover and roast in a 350–400°F. (180–200°C) oven about 1½ hours. (This takes the place of browning in fat.) Let pan cool, then refrigerate overnight. Meanwhile, soak beans overnight in water to cover.

Next day, drain beans, cover with fresh water and add the salt. Bring to a boil and simmer gently about 1 hour. Let cool, then drain — they should not be mushy.

Take shanks and separate meat from bones, leaving it in large chunks and reserving bones. Remove and discard fat in casserole, but leave the browned meat juices. Sauté the green onions in oil or pan fat in frying pan; then add tomatoes, mix well, and turn everything into the casserole.

Add drained beans, wine, lemon rind, oregano and a little pepper. Stir gently to mix, then add meat and bones — they add flavor. Don't worry about what looks like a lot of liquid. It will be absorbed.

Bake covered in a 350°F. (180°C) oven 1 hour, then discard bones, sprinkle with parsley and serve from the casserole. *Serves 6.*

Oven-Braised Fore Shanks

I like to bake these in an oval or long earthenware casserole with a tight-fitting cover (or foil). No basting is necessary. The result is superb.

4 lamb fore shanks
3 tbsp. (50 mL) melted lamb fat or vegetable oil
1 tsp. (5 mL) curry powder
1 tsp. (5 mL) brown sugar
1 tsp. (5 mL) salt
1½ cups (375 mL) lamb broth, red wine or water

Brown the shanks all over in the melted fat. Place in the bottom of the casserole. Sprinkle with the curry, sugar and salt. Pour the liquid in the bottom of the casserole, and cover tightly. Bake 2½ hours in a 250°F. (120°C) oven. *Serves 4*.

Thornbury Lamb Stew

Who was the first person to add orange flavoring to a lamb stew? We don't know, but we do find it in the French Provençal Daube, as well as in this world-famous stew which hails from Surrey, England.

4–6 lamb fore shanks
¼ lb. (0.15 kg) bacon
2 medium onions, chopped fine
2 cloves garlic, minced
1½ cups (375 mL) dry red wine
¼ tsp. (1 mL) rosemary
½ tsp. (2 mL) thyme
1 tsp. (5 mL) pepper
Thinly sliced rind of 1 orange
6–8 carrots, cut in 2 in. (5 cm) lengths

Dice the bacon, and cook in heavy metal saucepan until crisp and brown. Remove from fat with a slotted spoon. Add the onion and garlic to the fat. When lightly browned, remove the onions, and add to the bacon. Brown the meat in the remaining fat, then add the bacon and onion, and the remaining ingredients except the carrots.

Cover and cook over medium heat until the meat is tender, from 1–2 hours. In the last 40 minutes of the cooking period, add the carrots, and continue cooking on low heat. *Serves 6-8.*

Crofter Boiled Fore Shanks

A "crofter" is a Scottish farmer. Their cooking is simple but has the freshness and flavor of the Scottish Highlands, which makes it quite special. This dish is served with boiled potatoes and caper sauce.

4–5 lamb foreshanks
2 cloves garlic, sliced
½ tsp. (2 mL) thyme
2 tsp. (10 mL) salt
½ tsp. (2 mL) pepper
1 bay leaf
4 onions, peeled and cut in half
8 cups (2 L) water

Place all the ingredients in a large saucepan. Bring to a fast rolling boil. Cover and simmer over low heat for 2 hours or until meat is tender.

Make the caper sauce as follows: Melt 2 tbsp. (30 mL) butter in saucepan. Add 2 tbsp. (30 mL) flour, stir together until well blended. Remove from heat, add 2 cups (500 mL) of cooking broth passed through a strainer. Stir constantly over medium heat until sauce is creamy. Add 1 tsp. (5 mL) fresh lemon juice and 3 to 4 tbsp. (50–60 mL) capers or finely chopped sour pickles. Taste for seasoning. Serve hot over meat and boiled potatoes. *Serves 6.*

Lamb Shank Casserole

A tasty casserole made with sweet potatoes.

> 6 lamb shanks, about 1 lb. (0.5 kg) each
> Flour for dredging
> Salt, pepper, paprika and thyme to taste
> 3 tbsp. (50 mL) vegetable oil or bacon fat
> ¼ cup (60 mL) lemon juice
> ¼ cup (60 mL) water
> 1 tbsp. (15 mL) sugar
> 4–6 bay leaves
> 6 medium sweet potatoes
> 1 medium onion, finely chopped
> 2 tbsp. (30 mL) brown sugar

Dredge lamb shanks in seasoned flour. Heat oil or fat, and add meat, browning well all over. Place in large casserole. Combine drippings with lemon juice, water, sugar and bay leaves, and pour this mixture over lamb. Cover and bake at 325°F. (165°C) for about 1½ hours, or until meat is tender.

Top lamb with cooked sweet potatoes, cut into quarters, and top potatoes with a mixture of chopped onion and brown sugar. Cover and bake 20 minutes longer, or until potatoes are hot. Place under broiler for 3 to 5 minutes for a brown crust. *Serves 4–6.*

Sherried Lamb Casserole

I like to make this for a buffet, served with barley or a buckwheat (kasha) pilaf, and coleslaw with sour cream. Be sure to use very dry sherry.

  4 lamb fore shanks, left whole or cut in half
  2 tbsp. (30 mL) butter
  1 tsp. (5 mL) salt
  ¼ tsp. (1 mL) pepper
  ¼ tsp. (1 mL) thyme
  2 large onions, sliced
  4–6 carrots, sliced
  ½ cup (125 mL) dry sherry

Brown the lamb in the butter overr high heat. Transfer to a casserole dish. Sprinkle with the salt, pepper and thyme. Put the onions in the remaining fat and stir over medium heat, until lightly browned. Spread onions over the lamb, then top with the carrot slices. Pour the sherry over everything. Cover tightly, and bake in a 350°F. (180°C) oven for 1½ hours, or until meat is tender. *Serves 4.*

Swedish Potted Fore Shanks

A meal-in-a-pot. Fresh dill is the real Swedish flavoring. When not available, dill seeds are satisfactory.

4 lamb fore shanks, cut in half
2 tbsp. (30 mL) flour
1 tsp. (5mL) salt
½ tsp. (1 mL) pepper
½ tsp. (1 mL) nutmeg
2 tbsp. (30 mL) lamb fat, melted
2 tbsp. (30 mL) fresh dill, or 1 tsp. (5 mL) dill seeds
3 cups (750 mL) cold water
8 small onions
6–8 whole carrots
2 potatoes, diced
½ cup (125 mL) light cream
1 tbsp. (15 mL) flour

Mix together the flour, salt, pepper and nutmeg. Melt in a saucepan the fat removed from the lamb. Roll the meat in the seasoned flour, then brown it in the melted fat. Add the dill and water. Bring to a boil and simmer over low heat until the meat is tender, approximately 1½ hours. Then add the onions, carrots and potatoes. Cover and cook for another 20 minutes, or until vegetables are tender.

Mix together the cream and flour, and add to the stew sauce, stirring constantly until it thickens. *Serves 6.*

Norwegian Lamb Casserole

When I was in Norway, I was told that this is a national dish. Enjoy it after skiing or skating as the Norwegians do.

2–4 lb. (1–1.5 kg) lamb necks
1 medium cabbage
1 cup (250 mL) diced celery
¼ cup (60 mL) chopped celery leaves
2 tsp. (10 mL) salt
1 tbsp. (15 mL) sugar
1/3 cup (80 mL) flour
Lamb broth or water
2 tbsp. (30 mL) whole black peppercorns

Cut and core cabbage into 1–in. (2.5 cm) wedges. In heavy enamel or cast-iron saucepan or Dutch oven, place a layer of meat. Top with some cabbage. Blend together the celery, celery leaves, salt, sugar and flour. Sprinkle one third of this mixture over the meat. Repeat with meat, cabbage and flavoring mixture, so that you have at least 3 layers of each. Wrap peppercorns in cheesecloth and push into middle of dish. Add enough bouillon or water to cover half the dish. Cover and bring to a boil. Then, simmer over low heat 1½ to 2 hours, or until meat is tender, and serve with boiled potatoes. *Serves 6*.

Scottish Lamb and Tomato Casserole

A country favorite in Scotland. Tasty pieces of meat surrounded by crusty-topped scalloped tomatoes

> 3 lb. (1.4 kg) lamb necks, sliced
> 2 tbsp. (30 mL) butter
> 2 medium onions, sliced
> 1 tsp. (5 mL) salt
> ¼ tsp. (1 mL) pepper
> ¼ tsp. (1 mL) allspice
> 1 19-oz. (540 mL) can tomatoes
> 2 tsp. (10 mL) sugar
> 2 cups (500 mL) small cubes of bread
> ½ tsp. (2 mL) salt
> ¼ tsp. (1 mL) dill seeds
> 1 tbsp. (15 mL) butter

Heat the butter in frying pan, add the onions, and stir until softened and light brown. Remove from pan to a large casserole. Brown the meat in the remaining fat and add to the onions. Sprinkle with 1 tsp. (5 mL) salt, pepper and allspice. Mix together sugar and tomatoes, and pour over the meat.

Combine the bread cubes, the ½ tsp. (2 mL) salt, and the dill seeds, and pour over the tomatoes. Dot with the butter. Bake uncovered in a preheated 350°F. (180°C) oven for 1 hour, then cover and bake another 40 minutes. *Serves* 6.

Lamb and Barley Stew

Slow cooking in the oven gives this stew a perfect blending of flavor. At its best when prepared with lamb necks, but foreshanks cut into individual pieces can also be used.

  2 lb. (1 kg) lamb necks, sliced 1 in. (2.5 cm) thick
  Salt and pepper to taste
  2 tbsp. (30 mL) flour
  2 tbsp. (30 mL) vegetable oil or margarine
  1 cup (250 mL) onions, chopped
  4 tomatoes, quartered
  2 bay leaves
  2 tbsp. (30 mL) pearl barley
  6 prunes, pitted (optional)
  1 clove garlic, minced
  1 tsp. (5 mL) paprika
  1 cup (250 mL) water
  2 tbsp. (30 mL) sour cream

Roll the lamb in flour, and salt and pepper. Brown in the oil or margarine over high heat. Add the onions, cover and simmer 10 minutes, stirring several times. Add the remaining ingredients, except the sour cream.

Bake in a 250°F. (120°C) oven for 3 to 4 hours. It is important that the stew cook slowly. When ready to serve, add the sour cream and mix thoroughly. *Serves 6.*

Lamb Neck Florentine

Basil, dry or fresh mint, and orange rind is a very special flavoring combination used by Florentine cooks when they barbecue or bake all cuts of lamb. This is especially good served with minted green peas and parsleyed rice.

2 lb. (1 kg) lamb necks, sliced
7½ oz. (220 mL) can tomato sauce
1 green pepper, diced
1 onion, diced
¼ tsp. (1 mL) basil
1 tsp. (5 mL) fresh or dried mint
Peel of 1 orange, grated
½ tsp. (2 mL) salt
¼ tsp. (1 mL) pepper
¼–½ cup (60-125 mL) Parmesan cheese, grated (optional)

Preheat the oven to 350°F. (180°C). Place the neck slices side by side in a shallow baking pan. Mix together the tomato sauce, green pepper, onion, basil, mint, orange peel, salt and pepper.

Pour the mixture over the meat and bake for 40-60 minutes, or until tender. Keep the pan covered for the first 20 minutes and baste the meat 3 or 4 times during the cooking period. Place the meat on a hot platter and sprinkle with the cheese. *Serves 6.*

Barbecued Lamb Necks

These are unusually delicious barbecued to a nice, crisp golden brown, over the charcoals — so meaty, yet so economical.

    2–3 lb. (1–1.5 kg) lamb necks
    ½ cup (125 mL) vegetable oil
    Juice of 1 lemon
    Grated rind of ½ lemon
    1 medium onion, thinly sliced

Mix together the oil, lemon juice and rind. Add the meat and toss in this mixture until well coated. Top with onion slices, separated into rings. Cover tightly and refrigerate 6 to 12 hours, turning once or twice during that period. Barbecue 3 in. (7.5 cm) from the hot coals, 6 to 8 minutes on each side. If possible turn only once. *Serves 4–5.*

8 Liver, Heart, Tongue and Kidneys

Dishes made from these parts of the lamb are not served as often as other cuts, so I hope the recipes that follow will show you how very economical they are, and that they can be a rewarding adventure in good eating.

While lamb liver is not quite as creamy in texture as calves liver, it is just as tender and tasty — and much less expensive, too.

Lamb hearts are small and very tender; they are delicious when stuffed, and braised or fried.

Lamb tongues are considered a delicacy, and rightly so. The only problem is that they are not always available, so when you *can* get them, they are an extra special treat.

Lamb kidneys are delicate in flavor, and are also regarded as a connoisseur's choice. Unfortunately, they too have become increasingly difficult to find. Lamb kidneys have a thin membrane surrounding them, and this should be peeled off before cooking; another part that should be removed is the little ball of fat on the underside, which is easy to cut away with kitchen shears. The kidneys may be left whole or split in half crosswise. It is important to remember that if they are overcooked, lamb kidneys can become hard and dry. So cook them quickly over medium-low heat, turning them only once, to keep their naturally good taste and texture.

Liver and Noodles Julienne

Perfect for a light dinner. Even those who do usually not care for liver will appreciate this one.

1 lb. (0.5 kg) lamb liver, thinly sliced
3 tbsp. (50 mL) flour
1 tsp. (5 mL) salt
¼ tsp. (1 mL) pepper
Pinch of thyme
3 tbsp. (50 mL) butter
1 tbsp. (15 mL) vegetable oil
½ cup (125 mL) chopped green onions
½ cup (125 mL) white wine or dry vermouth
1 cup (250 mL) commercial sour cream
3 tbsp. (50 mL) parsley

Slice the liver as thinly as possible. Cut each slice in strips ½-in. (1.25 cm) wide. Place the flour, salt, pepper and thyme in a paper or plastic bag. Add the liver and shake the bag to coat the liver thoroughly with the flour.

Heat the butter and oil in a frying pan. Add the floured liver and stir over high heat for 2 minutes.

Place the liver on a hot platter. Add the green onions to the remaining fat and fry 2 or 3 minutes over medium heat. Pour the wine or vermouth in the frying pan; bring to a boil, then add the cream and parsley. Stir rapidly and remove from heat. The sauce should not boil after adding the cream. Pour over the liver and serve surrounded with well-drained, boiled noodles. *Serves 4.*

Broiled Lamb Liver

Hash browned potatoes are all that is needed with broiled liver for a quick, healthy meal.

1 lb. (0.5 kg) lamb liver thinly sliced
3 tbsp. (50 mL) butter or margarine
2 tbsp. (30 mL) onion, minced
2 tbsp. (30 mL) lemon juice
A pinch thyme or marjoram
Flour
Salt and pepper, and paprika to taste
Parsley

Melt the butter and add the onion; simmer over low heat for 5 to 10 minutes, stirring often. Remove from heat and add the lemon juice, thyme or marjoram.

Season the flour with the salt, pepper and paprika. Roll the lamb liver in this mixture and then in the buttered onions.

Place the liver slices side by side in the broiler tray (without the grill). Pour the remaining onion-butter sauce around the liver. Broil 3 to 4 in. (7.5–10 cm) from direct heat, for 3 to 5 minutes in all, turning only once. Baste twice during the cooking period. Sprinkle with parsley when done, and serve immediately. *Serves 4.*

Victorian Roasted Lamb Liver

A whole lamb's liver weighs about a 1 lb. (0.5 kg) or a little more. They are delectable served as a roast, and equally good served hot or cold (thinly sliced). The use of "bottled" sauces and port wine as flavoring gives this dish its Victorian heritage.

> 1–1½ lb. (0.5–0.75 kg) whole lamb liver
> 3 tbsp. (50 mL) butter
> 1 large onion, sliced
> 2 tbsp. (30 mL) green or red pepper, cut in slivers
> 2 tbsp. (30 mL) chili sauce
> 1 tbsp. (15 mL) A-1 sauce
> 1 tsp. (5 mL) each salt and pepper
> ¼ tsp. (1 mL) thyme
> ⅓ cup (80 mL) dry port wine
> ¼ cup (60 mL) hot or cold tea

Melt the butter in a frying pan. Add the onion and fry until golden brown. Add the green or red pepper, and stir over medium heat for 2 minutes. Remove from heat, and add chili and A-1 sauces, salt, pepper and thyme. Stir the whole mixture for a few seconds over medium heat.

Place liver in a baking dish. (Do not use too large a dish or the sauce around the liver will dry up.) Pour mixture on top of meat. Warm up the port wine in the sauce that you used for the vegetables, and pour around the liver.

Cook uncovered in a preheated 350°F. (175°C) oven for 50 minutes. Turn off oven, and let liver stand in oven for 15 minutes before removing. Then add the tea to the sauce in the dish, and baste the liver with this mixture 10–12 times. *Serves 6.*

Lamb Liver Venetian

Prepare everything needed beforehand. Then in 4 minutes, this dish is ready to serve. This is important because it should be served immediately.

   1 lb. (0.5 kg) lamb liver
   4 tbsp. (60 mL) butter
   2 cups (500 mL) onions, thinly sliced
   1 tsp. (5 mL) salt
   ¼ tsp. (1 mL) pepper
   2 tbsp. (30 mL) white wine or lemon juice
   1 tbsp. (15 mL) parsley

Using a very sharp knife, slice the lamb liver as thinly as possible on the bias. Then cut each slice in strips ½-in. (1.25 cm) wide. Melt the butter in a frying pan, and brown the onions.

Raise the heat to high. Add the liver all at once, and sauté for 3 minutes, stirring all the time. Add salt and pepper, the onions, and the wine or lemon juice. Simmer for 1 minute. Sprinkle with chopped parsley and serve. *Serves 4.*

Curried Shoulder Lamb Chops
Thick shoulder chops or large squares of boned shoulder are the best cuts to use to make a lamb curry.

French Lamb Navarin
This interesting classic of French cuisine is made from fresh lamb shoulder cut into cubes. Nutmeg is the secret of its intriguing flavor.

Sautéed Lamb Hearts

Serve with heavily parsleyed mashed potatoes and a glass of dry red wine and a green salad or buttered fresh spinach.

4–5 lamb hearts
2 tbsp. (30 mL) butter or margarine
3 green onions, finely chopped
1 clove garlic, chopped fine
2 tbsp. (30 mL) dry Madeira, sherry or water
½ tsp. (2 mL) tarragon or basil or sage
Salt and pepper to taste

Clean and cut hearts in ⅛-in. (0.32 cm) thick slivers. Melt the butter or margarine in a cast-iron frying pan until a nutty brown color. Add the meat all at once, stir constantly over high heat for 3 minutes, then remove to a hot platter. Add the green onions and garlic to the pan, and toss and stir for 1 minute. Remove the pan from the heat, and add the remaining ingredients. Return the meat to the pan, salt and pepper it again, and toss together over medium heat for a maximum of 2 minutes. Serve piping hot. *Serves 6.*

Pickled Lamb Tongues

Leave the small tongues whole. To bottle, use tall glass jar or turn tongue in half-moon shape in smaller jar. Will keep for months refrigerated.

6–8 lamb tongues
3 peppercorns
6 whole cloves
2 tsp. (10 mL) salt
2 bay leaves
½ cup (125 mL) white or cider vinegar

Cover the lamb tongues with hot water and simmer for 1 hour. Add the remaining ingredients. Cover and simmer until the tongues are tender, about 30–45 minutes more.

Let cool in the broth. Peel and clean. Leave whole or cut in pieces. Place in sterilized jars.

Skim fat off the broth. Pass through strainer and bring to a boil. Pour boiling hot broth over the tongues. Seal and refrigerate. *Yield: 1 pint (0.5 L).*

Curried Kidneys Dover Style

This is a good way to serve four people with four lamb kidneys. In a small, unusual restaurant in Dover, England, where I first ate them, they were served in piping hot puff pastry shells, along with small bamboo skewers holding crisp hot rolled pieces of bacon.

4 lamb kidneys
2 tbsp. (30 mL) butter
6 green onions or French shallots, finely chopped
1 tsp. (5 mL) curry powder
3 tbsp. (50 mL) flour
1 cup (250 mL) lamb or chicken broth
Salt and pepper to taste
2 tbsp. (30 mL) vodka or whisky
8 slices bacon (optional)

Cut kidneys into small bite-size pieces. Heat the butter in an enamel cast-iron pan. Or use a copper chafing dish, as it was done for us in Dover, set on a beautiful copper tray with another tray filled with the necessary ingredients. To the hot butter, add the green onions or French shallots, and stir until warm and bubbly. Add the curry powder and cook over low heat, stirring about 5 minutes. Roll the diced kidney in the flour and add to curry mixture, cook over medium heat, stirring most of the time, until they lose their red color. Add the lamb or chicken broth, and salt and pepper to taste. Simmer until sauce is creamy and kidneys are tender, about 10 minutes. Add the vodka or whisky, stir to mix, and serve.

If you wish to use the bacon, cook it on one side only, turn it over, and then remove it to absorbent paper to cool. Spread the uncooked side of each slice with a bit of chutney, and roll it, securing it with a small bamboo skewer. Place these on top of curried kidneys. *Serves 4.*

Lamb Kidneys Dijonnaise

Whenever possible, buy lamb kidneys that are still covered in their fat; they keep fresh 2 to 3 days longer than otherwise. When you do remove the fat, dice it and use it in cooking. To keep it for future use, melt it over low heat, then strain through a fine sieve, and refrigerate. When you have enough, try using it to make French fried potatoes — they will be really crisp and tasty.

1 lb. (0.5 kg) lamb kidneys (about 4) without fat
2 tbsp. (30 mL) butter or vegetable oil
1 tbsp. (15 mL) diced kidney fat (when available)
1 medium onion, thinly sliced
4-6 large mushrooms, sliced
1 tsp. (5 mL) dry mustard
1 tbsp. (15 mL) consommé or water
3 tbsp. (50 mL) flour
⅛ tsp. (.5 mL) tarragon
1 cup (250 mL) consommé
3 tbsp. (50 mL) commercial sour cream
1 tbsp. (15 mL) dry sherry or port
1 tsp. (5 mL) Dijon mustard

Cut kidney into thin slices. Melt the butter and kidney fat or oil. When very hot, add the kidneys and stir over high heat for 2 minutes. Remove from fat with a slotted spoon.

To the fat remaining in the pan, add the sliced onion, stir for 2 to 3 minutes or until light brown here and there, add the mushrooms and the dry mustard. Stir to mix, and add the 1 tbsp. (15 mL) of consommé or water. Stir over medium heat for 2 minutes. Add the flour and tarragon, and stir until well blended. Add the 1 cup (250 mL) of consommé, and stir over medium heat until creamy. Add the sour cream, dry sherry and Dijon mustard. Simmer 5 to 8 minutes over very low heat, stirring often. Add salt and pepper to taste. Serve in a nest of mashed potatoes or in a ring of buttered rice. *Serves 4.*

Lamb Kidneys Flambé

My husband's favorite. These should be served on toast, and you have a choice — be spectacular and flambé this dish with flair and flashes of bright light or just add the brandy and forget the flambé.

> 4 lamb kidneys
> 2 tbsp. (30 mL) butter
> 1 tsp. (5 mL) Dijon mustard
> ¼ tsp. (1 mL) salt
> 1 egg yolk
> 2 tbsp. (30 mL) cream
> Lemon juice to taste
> 2 tbsp. (30 mL) brandy

Slice the kidneys crosswise. Melt butter in a cast-iron frying pan until a nutty brown color, add kidneys and sauté over medium heat until lightly browned. Add mustard and salt, and stir to blend.

Beat egg yolk with cream and add a spoonful of sauce from frying pan. Turn heat down very low, add egg-cream mixture, remove from heat and stir to blend, then sprinkle with a bit of lemon juice.

Pour brandy into a large spoon, and set spoon directly on top of meat to heat, light brandy, and pour over kidneys. Or just pour brandy on kidneys and stir. *Serves 2–3.*

Pan-Fried Lamb Kidneys

My husband's favorite breakfast. I prepare the kidneys, ready to place in hot butter, the night before, and keep them refrigerated. The result is a quick super breakfast.

4–6 lamb kidneys
Red wine or cider vinegar
Prepared mustard or chutney
1 tbsp. (15 mL) bacon fat or butter
Salt and pepper
1 tsp. (5 mL) water

Remove outer membrane from the kidneys. Leave whole or halve lengthwise. Rub the kidneys with vinegar, then brush with prepared mustard or chutney.

Melt the fat in a frying pan, when lightly colored, add the kidneys and brown. Cook over medium-high heat 3 minutes on each side.

Salt and pepper to taste, and set on a hot plate. Add the water, to the fat in the frying pan, and stir for a few seconds before serving. *Serves 2.*

Lamb Kidneys Turbigo

This was the first luncheon dish I had to cook for my teacher when I was studying with Pellaprat at the Cordon Bleu cooking school in France. I have always enjoyed making it, and I serve it on *petits pains dorés* (little golden breads) as I did then.

> 8 lamb kidneys
> 3 tbsp. (50 mL) butter
> 12 cocktail sausages
> 12 small white onions
> 6 large mushrooms, quartered
> ½ tsp. (2 mL) tomato paste
> 2 tsp. (10 mL) arrowroot or all-purpose flour
> 1 cup (250 mL) chicken broth
> ¼ cup (60 mL) dry red wine
> 2 tbsp. (30 mL) sherry
> Salt and pepper to taste
> Minced chives or parsley

Skin the kidneys if they do not already have their skins removed. Remove center core and cut in half lengthwise. Heat the butter in a cast-iron frying pan. When it is sizzling, add the kidneys (cut side down, to seal the juices in), and brown quickly on both sides. Remove to a plate. Add the cocktail sausages to the remaining butter, brown lightly and remove from pan with a slotted spoon. Add the small onions, and stir over low heat until well coated with the fat, and simmer over low heat for 10 to 15 minutes or until they are just tender. They must remain a bit crunchy. Add the mushrooms and stir the whole mixture together.

Blend together the tomato paste, flour and red wine. Add this to onion-mushroom mixture, then add the chicken broth and the sherry, and stir over medium heat until mixture comes to a boil and the sauce is light and creamy. Put kidney and sausages back into the sauce, and simmer until hot. Serve on toast or in golden bread.

To prepare the "golden bread," cut 8 rounds or squares of bread (without crusts) 2-in. (5 cm) in diameter and ½ in. (1.25 cm) thick. Fry slowly in 3 tbsp. (50 mL) butter, turning them to brown them all over. These can be made in advance and warmed up in a 300°F. (150°C) oven just before serving. *Serves 8.*

9   *Leftovers*

Since life is demanding, help scarce, time fleeting, and food so costly, leftovers can help us cope with all we have to do. Of course, we know that short cuts and instant foods are "king." But we often by-pass leftovers, foods that carry no actual price tag at all, foods that can become quick, no-expense meals with a few minutes in the kitchen. You may cook a stew, freeze the leftovers in a freezer-to-oven dish, and later all you need to do is place the dish in the oven, heat and serve.

Leftover lamb can be quickly transformed into many delicious and elegant dishes — a **French Lamb Salad**, a **Dorset Cold Lamb Platter**, or **Lamb-Stuffed Green Peppers** — and can be a breakthrough in "fast foods" in your kitchen. Try them!

How to Serve a Cold Leg of Lamb

Remove the leg of lamb from the refrigerator at least 4 hours before serving. Slice as thinly as possible, and remove all the fat.

Serve with mayonnaise mixed with prepared mustard — ½ cup (125 mL) mayonnaise for 2 tbsp. (30 mL) mustard — and a green salad or potato salad.

Lamb Roast Kebabs

Delicious for a snack or as a luncheon dish, served with a salad.

        Cold lamb roast
        Sweet pickles
        1 cup (250 mL) sour cream
        ½ cup (125 mL) carrots
        1 tbsp. (15 mL) grated onion

Cut the lamb in 1-in. (2.5 cm) cubes, and chop the pickles in ½-in. (1.25 cm) pieces. Make small kebabs, alternating the lamb and pickles on skewers. Serve cold, dipping the skewers in the following sauce.

Sauce: Mix together in a bowl the sour cream, grated carrot and onion, and refrigerate for 1 hour before serving. *Yield: Enough sauce for 16 kebabs.*

Dorset Cold Lamb Platter

Dorset, England, is famous for its sheep. The following cold cut plate is most attractive, unusual and so tasty. A perfect way to serve cold roast of lamb.

> 10–12 slices cooked lamb
> ¼ cup (60 mL) fresh mint, chopped fine
> ¼ cup (60 mL) cider or wine vinegar
> ¼ cup (60 mL) sugar
> ¼ cup (60 mL) water
> ½ tsp. (2 mL) salt
> ¼ tsp. (1 mL) pepper
> Shredded iceberg lettuce
> Sliced tomatoes
> 4 tbsp. (60 mL) mayonnaise
> 2 tbsp. (30 mL) chutney

Combine mint, vinegar, sugar, water, salt and pepper. Stir until the sugar is dissolved. Cover and let rest at room temperature 3 to 6 hours before using.

Slice lamb thinly (out of refrigerator 3 to 6 hours before serving). Set on a platter. Pour some of the mint sauce over it. Surround with the shredded lettuce and tomatoes.

Serve with the rest of the mint sauce and the mayonnaise mixed with the chutney. *Yield: enough sauce for 10–12 slices of lamb.*

Lamb Hash

This recipe is a variation of a traditional Quebec dish, and is a favorite in our family — we serve it with mashed potatoes.

    3 cups (750 mL) diced cooked lamb
    1 onion, finely chopped
    2 tbsp. (30 mL) butter or melted lamb fat
    1 tbsp. (15 mL) minced parsley or celery leaves
    1 cup 250 mL) diced cooked potatoes
    7½ oz. (210 mL) can tomato sauce
    1 cup (250 mL) leftover lamb gravy or
        ½ cup (125 mL) water
    Salt and pepper to taste
    ½ tsp. (2 mL) thyme

Brown the onion lightly in the butter or fat. Add the parsley (or celery leaves), tomato sauce, gravy (or water), salt, pepper and thyme. Bring to a boil and simmer for 10 minutes.

Add the lamb, and cover and simmer over low heat for 1 hour, or bake in a 350°F. (180°C) oven for 35 minutes. *Serves 4.*

Réchauffé Lamb Stew

In the Victorian age, a dish had flair when part of its name was taken from the French, such as *réchauffé*, which means "warmed up." And that is just what happens to the cooked lamb in this old recipe.

    2 cups (500 mL) diced, cooked lamb
    1 onion, coarsely chopped
    2/3 cup (165 mL) chopped celery
    1 tsp. (5 mL) salt
    ¼ tsp. (1 mL) pepper
    Grated peel of ½ a lemon
    ⅛ tsp. (0.5 mL) thyme
    1 cup (250 mL) potatoes, cooked and diced
    2/3 cup (165 mL) canned tomatoes
    1/3 cup (80 mL) chopped green pepper (optional)
    1 cup (250 mL) any bouillon or lamb stock

Put the lamb in a 1½-quart (1½ L) baking dish, add remaining ingredients, and bake in a 300°F. (150°C) oven for 20 minutes. Top casserole with a layer of your favorite biscuit mix, and bake another 20 minutes at 400°F. (200°C) or until biscuits are golden brown. *Serves 4.*

Lamb-Stuffed Green Peppers

This dish, adapted from the cooking of Southern Italy, is equally good served hot or cold.

    1 cup (250 mL) cooked lamb, chopped fine
    4 green peppers
    1 small onion, chopped
    1 tbsp. (15 mL) fat
    ¼ cup (60 mL) water
    2 fresh tomatoes, diced
    ½ cup (125 mL) cooked rice
    Salt and pepper to taste
    Pinch of basil
    ½ cup (125 mL) water
    1 tsp. (5 mL) sugar
    1 tbsp. (15 mL) olive oil, butter or other fat

Slice off the top of each pepper, remove the seeds and ribs. Place in a saucepan of boiling water, blanch them for 5 minutes, then drain on an absorbent paper.

Fry the onion in the fat, add the ¼ cup (60 mL) water, diced tomatoes, basil, salt, pepper and lamb. Simmer for 10 minutes, then stir in the rice.

Stuff the peppers with the lamb mixture, and place in a baking dish. Pour the ½ cup (125 mL) water in the bottom, and add the sugar and the fat. Bake in a 350°F. (180°C) oven for 35 to 40 minutes. *Serves 4.*

Fricandeau of Lamb

The French way to make patties with cooked meat.

> 2–3 cups (500–750 mL) cooked lamb
> 2 thick slices stale bread
> 2 tbsp. (30 mL) milk
> A fresh tomato, diced
> 1 small onion, chopped fine
> 1 beaten egg
> Salt, pepper and nutmeg to taste
> Breadcrumbs to coat
> Fat to brown

Soak the bread in the milk, and work into a thick paste with a fork.
Add the cooked ground lamb, the tomatoes, onion and beaten egg. Add salt, pepper and nutmeg, and shape into patties. Roll in bread crumbs, then brown in the fat over medium heat for 2 or 3 minutes. *Serves 2–4.*

Leftover Lamb with Sauerkraut

If you like sauerkraut, you will appreciate this Bavarian way of reheating lamb. They serve this dish with boiled potatoes rolled in chopped parsley.

> 2–3 cups (500–750 mL) diced cooked lamb
> 4 slices bacon
> 1 onion, minced
> 3–4 cups (750–1000 mL) sauerkraut
> Salt and pepper to taste
> 1 tsp. (5 mL) anise

Fry the bacon, and then brown the onion in the bacon fat. Add the sauerkraut, salt, pepper and anise. Cover and simmer for 1 hour. Add the lamb, cover and simmer for another 15 minutes. *Serves 4.*

Creamy Lamb Fricassée

The can of cream of celery soup makes this a quick and easy dish.

1½–2 cups (375–500 mL) cooked lamb, diced
¼ cup (60 mL) margarine
1 large onion, chopped fine
3 cups (750 mL) cooked and diced potatoes
1 can cream of celery soup, undiluted
½ tsp. (2 mL) savory or dill

Melt the margarine in a frying pan, and lightly brown the onions and potatoes for approximately 10 minutes.

Add the rest of the ingredients and mix well. Cover and simmer 15 minutes over low heat, stirring occasionally. Taste for seasoning, and serve. *Serves 4.*

Lamb Broth

Bones from 2–3 lb. (1–1.5 kg) lamb-in-the-basket
4 cups (1 L) water
1 unpeeled onion, cut in four
1 unpeeled clove of garlic, cut in half
1 bay leaf
10 peppercorns
A few celery leaves or a stick of celery, coarsely chopped
1 tsp. (5 mL) coarse salt
½ tsp. (2 mL) thyme

Add all ingredients to the pot, and bring to a fast rolling boil. Cover and simmer 1½ hours. Cool for 3 to 6 hours, then strain.

If you prefer a fat-free stock, wait until it has cooled, then place it in a bowl, cover and refrigerate overnight. The fat will rise to the top and harden. It is then very easy to remove in one piece.

Garnish to taste or use for any recipe requiring stock. *Yield: 4 cups (1 L).*

Cream of Barley Soup

Use the **Lamb Broth** recipe to prepare this thick creamy soup. *Grand-maman* used to call it "my most painless soup." In the winter she made it in large quantities and buried it in the snow with coarse salt spread around it here and there, the same as we still do for ice cream.

4–6 cups (1–1.5 L) lamb broth
3 tbsp. (50 mL) butter (do not use other fat)
½ cup (125 mL) pot barley
1 celery stalk with leaves, finely chopped
1 large onion, finely chopped
½ tsp. (2 mL) dill seeds or summer savory
Salt and pepper to taste
1 cup (250 mL) light cream

Heat the butter in a saucepan, and add the barley, celery, onion, and dill seeds or summer savory. Stir most of the time over medium heat, 5 to 6 minutes or until barley is golden brown. Add the lamb broth and salt and pepper to taste. Bring to a fast rolling boil, cover and simmer over very low heat for 40 to 60 minutes. Cool and purée in a blender. (My *grand-maman* used to pass it through a *Chinois*, still used today by professional chefs. This is a fine, cone-shaped strainer, with a wooden mallet, used to roll around in it.)

Pour the soup back into the saucepan, and bring to a boil over low heat. Add the cream, and heat through, but do not let it boil. *Serves 4–6.*

French Lamb Salad

A very interesting way to serve leftover lamb. In French cuisine, they usually pour hot consommé over the cooked meat when using it for a salad. The salt pork crackling can be replaced by bacon.

> 3 cups (750 mL) diced cooked lamb
> ½ cup (125 mL) warm consommé
> 2 tbsp. (30 mL) cider vinegar
> 4 tbsp. (60 mL) vegetable oil
> 1 tsp. (5 mL) salt
> 1 tbsp. (15 mL) chopped fresh parsley
> ¼ tsp. (1 mL) tarragon or basil
> ½ cup (125 mL) diced salt pork
> 1 cup (250 mL) cooked long grain rice
> Thinly sliced cucumber

Combine the consommé, vinegar, oil, salt, parsley and basil in a salad bowl, and stir until thoroughly mixed. Sauté the diced salt pork until you have crisp, brown crackling. Pour off the rendered fat (save for other uses), and drain crackling on paper towels.

Add rice and lamb to dressing in bowl. Toss together, and add pork crackling. Mix again and top salad with several cucumber slices. Do not refrigerate since this salad is best at room temperature. *Serves 6.*

Cold Tongue Salad

A welcome summer dish.

> 2 cups (500 mL) cold, cooked lamb tongue
> ½ cup (125 mL) French dressing
> 1 unpeeled apple, diced
> 1 cup (250 mL) celery, diced
> ¼ tsp. (1 mL) curry powder

Cut tongue in thin slices, and marinate for 1 hour in the French dressing.

Then add the remaining ingredients, and toss together. Serve on raw spinach leaves or over chopped green cabbage (without dressing because there is already enough on the tongue). Sprinkle a few chopped walnuts over the salad. *Serves 2–3.*

10

Cooking Lamb Outdoors: The Méchoui

Méchoui (or *michwi*) is an Arabic word meaning "to roast," and it is used especially when referring to the roasting of a whole young lamb outdoors on a spit or grill over a charcoal or wood fire. For Arabs, the *méchoui* is considered the very best way to serve lamb, which is their most important meat.

Méchoui barbecue parties are becoming more and more popular in North America, and are thorougly enjoyable occasions. If you would like to try a *méchoui*, go ahead — the equipment you'll need is quite simple, and it is easy to do once you are organized.

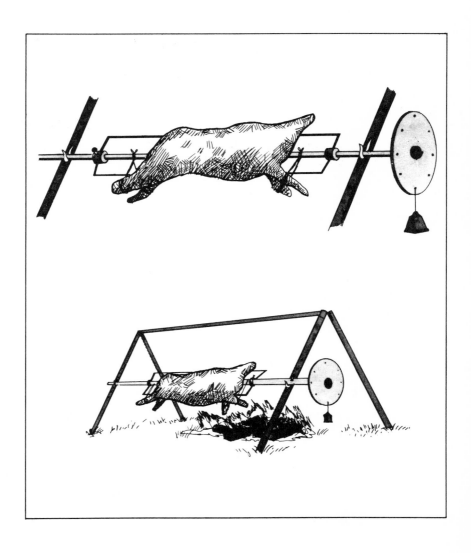

1. *The Fire:*

The outdoor fire for the *méchoui* must be red hot, and the coals topped with white ashes before you start to roast. When making an efficient turnspit, keep these points in mind: The spit must be set at a level which allows the meat to turn in front of the fire, and at the right distance from it, 3 to 3½ ft. (90–105 cm). Also, make sure that there are air vents to the ash pit, drip pans set low enough to prevent the drippings from being burned, and a piece of metal placed beside the fire to keep the heat in and prevent live coals from falling into the drippings. If you give careful attention to these details before you start cooking, then the rest is easy.

The fire itself is best made on old furnace bars or a piece of an old iron fence placed at least 1 ft. (30 cm) off the ground, and built up on this at least 2 ft. (60 cm) high, so that the heat radiates onto the carcass as it is slowly turned. The spit can consist of a long galvanized pipe, 1½ in. (3.75 cm) in diameter, with a sturdy old cartwheel or round metal circle with holes punched in it, and a weight fixed to it. A peg is inserted into a hole and held in place with a piece of wire. The spit is then set in hooks on top of a metal bar at not more than 3 ft. (90 cm) above the drip pan. The lamb carcass is impaled on the pipe, and is rotated back and forth (every 20 minutes or so) during the cooking period by an operator who stands to one side of the fire, out of the direct line of heat. The operator turns the carcass by removing the peg, and turning the wheel a quarter of a turn, then reinserting the peg.

2. *The Drip Pan:*

Make this with a double or triple layer of aluminum foil no larger or longer than necessary to catch the juices. Use a straight edge, such as a wooden board, to help fold the sides of the foil evenly; then crimp the corners to make them secure. Heavy-duty foil is the best kind to use. Set the pan directly under the lamb.

3. *The Wire Basket:*

If the lamb is cut into quarters or individual pieces for roasting, then a large type of wire broiler can be used. These "baskets" are available where barbecue equipment is sold. The cuts are placed side by side in the basket, the meat brushed on both sides with the basting sauce given on page 122. The basket can be placed on top of a 3-sided wall of stones about 2 ft. (60 cm) high. Use a drip pan as above.

Before a barbecue, you should light the fire and make a complete test of the set-up — for shielding the wind, the type of fuel being used, the efficiency of the turning wheel, and so on. The fire should be started early enough, so that it is sufficiently burned to give an even flow of heat along the full length of the turnspit. Later, as the lamb is being roasted, the heat of the fire must be reduced at the fore quarter end, or it will be done before the thicker hind quarter is cooked. Essential to a good spit roasting is constant basting. Use ladles or basting spoons firmly fastened to long poles for this purpose.

4. The Lamb:

Have the butcher prepare a whole young lamb, weighing about 30 to 40 lb. (15–20 kg) dressed. This will serve about 20–25 people. Make sure the butcher cuts only a 12 to 14 in. (30–35 cm) opening in the middle of the stomach. If you have the facilities, hang the carcass by a large hook in a cool place, for no longer than 48 hours. If you do not have a suitable place to hang the lamb, place it in the refrigerator for the same amount of time.

Sponge the lamb inside and out with a cloth dipped in a mixture of half cider or wine vinegar and half water, than pat dry with paper towels. Crush 10 to 12 cloves of unpeeled garlic together with 3 tbsp. (50 mL) coriander seeds and 5 tbsp. (75 mL) coarse salt; do this with the ingredients wrapped in a cloth, and crush them with a heavy knife or a stone as the Arabs do. Pour mixture into the stomach of the lamb, and add 2 tsp. (10 mL) freshly ground pepper, 2 lemons, unpeeled and sliced and ½ lb. (0.5 kg) margarine in one piece.

Tie up the opening with a piece of soft wire. I like to use florist's wire because it is easy to manipulate, but any wire can be used. (Don't use string or thread since they will burn during the roasting.)

Push the metal rod through the lamb carcass from head to hind quarter, and truss the legs together with wire, attaching them to the rod, and set the rod on the spit. Then rub the outside of the lamb all over with 1 lb. (0.5 kg) margarine creamed with 2 tbsp. (30 mL) paprika, and 2 tbsp. (30 mL) each thyme and ground cumin.

Basting Sauce: Melt an additional 1 lb. (0.5 kg) margarine, and add the juice of 2 lemons and 1 tbsp. (15 mL) thyme, and use this to baste the meat. When

I have fresh thyme, I tie large bouquet of it around the cloth part of a clean dishmop, and use that to dip in the basting sauce, brushing a bit on the lamb each time it is turned (about every 15 to 20 minutes).

Build a bed of red-hot coals thick enough to last 3 to 4 hours. Suspend the lamb on the spit in front of the coals, as shown in the illustration. Place the large drip pan of heavy-duty foil under the lamb to catch the drippings, which are used for gravy.

It usually takes 3 hours to slowly barbecue the lamb. When it is ready, it should be golden brown and crisp on the outside, and the meat should be very juicy on the inside. When it is ready to serve, remove the wire from the opening, and pour the juices into the drip pan (two people are needed to do this); then pour the contents of the drip pan into a large, hot saucepan. Add to this 2 cans of undiluted consommé and, if you like, 2 cups (500 mL) dry Madeira wine or 1 cup (250 mL) rye whisky. Let the mixture get hot, while you scrape the bottom of the drip pan; add any more drippings to the mixture in the saucepan. Serve very hot; this is easy to do by reheating over hot charcoals, if necessary.

To serve, get a good carver to do the cutting of the meat. Remove the lamb from the rod to a large table covered with oilcloth or a large wooden board; put a hot platter beside the lamb on which to place the slices of meat. Everyone helps themselves from the platter, and enjoys the delicate flavor that only a *méchoui* can give to lamb.

The Moroccans set bowls of coarse salt mixed with ground cumin on the table, and dip their pieces of meat into it — 2 tbsp. (30 mL) salt to 1 tbsp. (15 mL) cumin. Perhaps you might enjoy this, too.

Mongolian Méchoui

I like to use this recipe when barbecuing quarters of lamb. I serve slices of hot, cooked lamb set on top of sesame rolls that have been split and toasted on the barbecue. When possible, get Armenian or Syrian sesame rolls — they're super.

    1 lamb carcass, quartered
    3 cups (750 mL) water
    2 tbsp. (30 mL) whole star anise
    1 tbsp. (15 mL) whole peppercorns
    ½ cup (125 mL) dry sherry or Sake wine
    ¼ cup (65 mL) Japanese soy sauce
    2 cups (500 mL) finely-chopped green onions
    1 cup (250 mL) chopped fresh parsley (use cilantro,
        often called Italian parsley, when available)

Barbecue the lamb, set in a wire basket. Brush the meat with melted margarine flavored with the grated rind of 1 lemon and 1 orange.

In a saucepan, bring to a boil the water, stir anise, and peppercorns, then simmer for 20 minutes. Add the remaining ingredients, and stir well. Keep hot; when ready to serve, carve a piece of cooked lamb, dip it into the hot flavored liquid, and place on an unbuttered roll.

When Mongolians serve this dish, they say, "May you enjoy it and be happy in your stomach."

Index